# WHILE EARTH STILL SPEAKS

# WHILE EARTH STILL SPEAKS

## Nancy Werking Poling

Screech Owl Press

Published by
Screech Owl Press.
Black Mountain, NC 28711

www.NancyPoling.com

In conjunction with:
Old Mountain Press
PO Box 66
Webster, NC 28788

# Also by Nancy Werking Poling

*Before It Was Legal: a black-white marriage (1945-1987)* the true story of a talented black man, an independent white woman, and the times in which these two remarkable people lived

*Had Eve Come First and Jonah Been a Woman*
a collection of short stories in which heroes of Hebrew Scripture are imagined as women

*Out of the Pumpkin Shell*
a novel about women's friendship and family secrets

*Victim to Survivor: women recovering from clergy sexual abuse*
Nancy Werking Poling, Editor

For Aliza, Azlynn, Carson, Jimmy, Madeleine, and Trey I bequeath to you a beautiful, wounded planet. May you have the courage and wisdom to help Earth and its creatures, including humans, survive. I love you all.

"One day some great opportunity stands before you and calls you to stand up for some great principle, some great issue, some great cause. And you refuse to do it because you are afraid.... You refuse to do it because you want to live longer.... Well, you may go on and live until you are 90, but you're just as dead at 38 as you would be at 90. And the cessation of breathing in your life is but the belated announcement of an earlier death of the spirit."

Martin Luther King Jr.<br>
Sermon, November 5, 1967, Ebenezer Baptist Church

# Chapter 1

**ROME**

L AGGING BEHIND A STREAM of disembarking passengers, Elizabeth envies their purposeful gaits, the confidence with which they pull their suitcases along Fiumicino's wide corridors. Garbled words in a language she doesn't understand blare over the P.A. system. She feels disoriented, alone. But at Customs a young man with dark curly hair and an olive complexion stamps her passport, smiles broadly, and says, "Benvenuto. I hope you enjoy our country." Returning his smile, she allows her shoulders to relax a little.

She has no plan, only a round-trip ticket. A suitcase packed with a loose-fitting dress made in Guatemala, a broomstick skirt, a pair of navy blue pants, four tops. Essential cosmetics. An extra supply of vitamins in case she's successful in her search and ends up staying longer. Maybe too, if she's unsuccessful but sufficiently optimistic. She wears white sneakers—comfortable footwear for extensive walking—and a wide-brimmed straw hat to protect her face from the harsh rays of the Italian sun.

Beyond the door marked *Uscita,* throngs of people stand behind a scarlet velvet rope, some with tear-filled eyes frantically waving, others holding up signs with neatly printed names. Briefly she's convinced she sees Angelica among the crowd. Even takes steps in that direction. Her heart wrenches. It can't be Angelica, she reminds herself. No one is here to greet her. She's on her own.

How foolish, especially at this age, to impulsively pack her suitcase and set her mind on a destination clear across the Atlantic. Foolish too to think Mary's final *ciao* carried significance. That the R picked at random from the Scrabble box indicated Rome. Yet some magnetic force, as irrational as it is, has drawn her to the Eternal City, offering no choice but to attach herself to this place at this time.

She lifts her chin, thrusts her shoulders back, and heads for the Information kiosk. Ten minutes later, one hand pulling her suitcase, the other clinging to maps and directions to her lodging, she follows signs to the subway.

THERE'S NO INDICATION this is her destination, no plaque signifying that behind these formidable stucco walls accommodations await travelers. Only a street number next to a doorway and a small white button. Which she pushes. A fuzzy voice speaking Italian comes from a metal box beside the wide door. She scrambles through the first few pages of her Italian-English dictionary.

"Non capisco," she says into the box. The fuzzy voice returns, words she doesn't understand race past her. Frantically, she turns more pages.

"Non parlo italiano."

Again the fuzzy voice.

"Non parlo italiano!" she yells in case she wasn't heard before.

A loud buzz. She jerks open the door, steps in, and is immediately forced to gaze upward into a large glass window with a cut-out circle the size of a saucer. On the other side of the glass, a wimple shrouds a face with the texture of corrugated cardboard. Like a deity, an elderly nun looms, her mouth against the opening. A mouth twisted in disapproval.

"Non parlo italiano," Elizabeth repeats, meekly this time.

"No speak italiano, no com'a Italia." The piercing eyes and firm jaw indicate the foreigner's patronage is not appreciated.

Elizabeth excuses the gruffness. Tells herself the nun was probably once an idealistic young woman, not unlike Angelica. Both responding to a call. No doubt the sister's was to heal the sick or teach the young. But the financial burdens of maintaining a decaying convent with flaking plaster and antiquated plumbing necessitate taking in tourists. Angelica has committed herself to a holy cause as well. She too, Elizabeth fears, will discover that the realities of commerce have a way of intruding on idealism. If she can stay alive.

ELIZABETH FOLLOWED INTERNET suggestions for avoiding jetlag: engaged in a cycle of fasting and feasting two days before leaving home, took Melatonin, wore a blindfold during the flight, consumed no caffeine, and walked up and down the aisles. To no avail.

3:00 a.m. She awakens to her first day in Rome. Back home it's nine in the evening, the hour when she usually lets Jezebel out one last time before climbing the stairs to her bedroom. She'd likely be drowsy right now had she not, immediately after arriving in this room, dropped onto the bed and fallen into a deep sleep.

3:30. She stands in the dark, gazing out the screenless, open-shuttered window. City lights veil the night sky. Lush tropical plants in the courtyard below cast amorphous shadows.

*Angelica. Heart of my heart. To lose you and Mary both... No, I refuse to be despondent. I refuse to be despondent. I will find Mary. I will find Mary. And I will get the answer I'm looking for. But what is the question? I don't even know what the question is.*

4:00. She turns on the only lamp, its single bulb of minimal wattage. A crucifix hangs above the narrow bed. A Bible rests on the night stand. It's a closet of a room, the facility recommended in *Economical Lodging in Italy's Convents*. From the book it seemed a peaceful oasis in the heart of the city. More like a tomb, it's turned out to be.

The kind of place where her father would have felt right at home—it's that depressing. A dreary and austere interior, long hallways of darkly stained wood. Certainly not the Hilton, but it's cheap and only two blocks from the subway. At least she has a private bathroom, the size of those found in camping trailers. A necessity for a woman whose bladder makes late-night demands.

5:00. No alarms go off as she slips out the front door into the final hours of darkness. Across the street two other pedestrians walk with resolve in the direction she's heading: toward Piazza Barberini, where yesterday, after lugging her suitcase up subway steps, she paused to catch her breath. Right in front of an all-night internet café.

This morning—or is it night? her body wants to know—she settles into a plastic chair in a narrow carrel and tentatively brings finger tips to computer keys. Only one of her messages sent from home has been answered: "I'm O.K."

*Encrypt* is the word Angelica used. Computer nerds, she promised, will work their magic, make sure the FBI can't trace communications.

> To: wl83@torbox3.onion                    Sept 21 5:31 AM
> Subject: Hello
> Dear One,
> I get a lump in my throat just thinking about you. I wonder where you are and constantly worry. I wish you'd consider how your decision affects those of us who love you. I'm sorry if that sound selfish.
>
> On top of fears about your safety, I'm upset because Mary left. It had nothing to do with the bishop declaring the apparitions invalid. "These women aren't going to rescue diddlysquat." That's what she told me.
>
> With you both gone, I feel abandoned and alone. I want things to be as they were, with you in school and Mary depending on me.
>
> You more than anyone understand how devastating this is. That's why I'm in Rome. Yes, Rome, Italy. I'm searching for her. I want to convince her to come back home with me, to not give up. As long as she and I work together, we can make it happen. I'm sure we can. She just didn't give our project enough time.
>
> I locked up the store and put a "Temporarily Closed" sign out front. I'll reopen when I get back. Hank's taking care of the farm. Timing couldn't be worse. My garden crew has already gone back to college, so there'll be

nobody to harvest the last of the tomatoes. What a waste, so many of them rotting on the vine.

Several nights I've had nightmares of you in a coffin. Instead of a complete body lying there, though, your limbs are scattered. I know it's morbid and I can hear you telling me, "I can handle this, Mom." Before, I could at least talk to Mary, who fully understands a mother's anxiety.

I'll keep repeating: please go back and finish your degree.

Love,
Mom

5:45. Elizabeth leans out the window of her room. From the chapel across the courtyard come the melodic strains of the sisters' morning hymns. Reminding her of mornings at the farm, the women stepping out of tents, voices raised in song as they formed a procession down to the pond.

6:30. She descends in the wobbly elevator barely large enough for her and the paunchy man with dark greasy hair and body odor. On the main floor she finds the nuns bustling about, their black habits swishing across glossy wood floors. Two give her cold stares but say nothing as she walks around, peering inside open doorways. In a narrow room with a dark green vinyl sofa and matching chair, apparently the sisters' notion of a lounge, she finds what she's looking for. But the reception, only in black and white, is limited to four channels, all of them fuzzy and in Italian. Briefly she panics. *Well, I'll just have to get news someplace else,* she tells herself.

7:00. Having already been awake four hours, she goes to breakfast in the convent dining room. What she read on the internet is confirmed: Italians start the day with little more than a cup of cappuccino and a crusty roll with butter and jelly.

8:00. She puts on her wide-brimmed straw hat and sets out to explore the neighborhood.

Streets running off Piazza Barberini are like spokes of a bicycle wheel that's been run over by a car. Directly behind the convent is Via Veneto, with its luxury hotels, where the more affluent stay. She enters the lobby of each with the confidence of a paying guest, sweeping into lounge areas with cushioned chairs, crystal chandeliers, and Italian statuary. Checking which ones have TVs tuned to English-speaking news channels.

And if by chance there's anything with ties to Angelica? At least the American Embassy is nearby. She tries not to nurture thoughts of what might go wrong.

IN AN OUTSIDE café overlooking Piazza Navona, supplementing breakfast at the convent with a cornetto, Elizabeth gazes out over the piazza crowded with tourists wearing shorts and visors. The sun's rays bounce off Bernini's Four Rivers Fountain, its four male figures lolling around a phallic obelisk affirming their manhood. Only briefly do their muscular biceps and thighs, their mostly uncovered bodies, hold her attention. Instead she studies mothers and fathers as they keep watch over children who run and squeal. It's a musical scene, the rhythms of cascading water accompanying the melody of children's laughter, the harmonizing of adults' animated conversation. An orchestra she's seldom felt part of, hers having been a life mostly out of sync, out of tune.

Families, all of them in high spirits, pose in front of cameras. A painful reminder of demands to keep her own family intact. But she could not stay. Not for them or the church, not for God. Wendell viewed it as one more embarrassment, a humiliation.

For Elizabeth it felt like life or death.

# Chapter 2

NOT UNTIL THE YEAR Wendell and I marked our twenty-seventh wedding anniversary, did I say to myself, *I wonder what happy feels like.* When I had such thoughts, a spectrum of hues fanned out in my mind. In Pulaski, I'd stop in front of a store window at the mall to take in the bright patterns on women's clothing and home decorating. What would it be like to live colorfully?

From the picture window of our Virginia farmhouse, I gazed out on the broad expanse of the valley, cattle grazing on knolls of emerald green pasture in the foreground, hazy mountain ridges far to the east. I lacked no necessities. The farm, in the Mattison family for three generations, produced a secure income that kept ample food on the table, a roof over our heads. There was no reason for discontent, I told myself.

But did my life have purpose? Of course, it did. I was the wife of a good man. Motherhood—I, more than most women, understood what a blessing it is to be a mother. After two miscarriages within the first ten years of marriage, Wendell and I gave up ever having children, only to be surprised the year I turned thirty-nine. I gave birth to Randy, then to Angelica three years later. Now Randy was active in his high school's chapter of Future Farmers of America, a good kid, though at a surly stage. A spittin' image of his dad, with a stocky build and eye brows scrunched toward each other in earnestness. Angelica had a circle of friends and excelled in her studies. An energetic girl, with auburn hair and freckles.

No small accomplishment, nurturing a family.

I tried to convince myself that I was merely going through what I'd heard referred to as a *mid-life crisis.*

~~~
~~~

ANGELICA STRAINED FORWARD against her seatbelt as if the tension would move us to our destination sooner.

"You know your father won't approve," I told her. "And he won't like me bringing you."

"But I've been taught to stand up for my beliefs," she said with righteous confidence. "Didn't Jesus ask, 'Who is my mother?' Some things are more important than worrying about what our parents think."

I took my eyes off the road, gave her the arched eyebrow. "But I tell you, Mary didn't appreciate it one bit, what he said….Uh, I *doubt* that she appreciated it."

An important correction. I'd never told anyone about our conversations, Mary's and mine. I wasn't even sure they'd really happened. Didn't *want* to believe they had. Time spent in the library as a teenager, reading psychology books with big words, convinced me that only mentally ill people heard voices, and more than anything I wanted to be normal.

Yet Angelica's remark reminded me: "Don't be like Yeshu," Mary once advised from the corner of my bedroom ceiling while I sulked over Mama reprimanding me. "I warned him to quit speaking out."

*Mothers don't forget,* I considered telling Angelica. Her father probably wouldn't either.

I pulled up to the curb in front of Williams' Seeds and Farm Supplies. A group of adolescents marched in a wide circle, carrying signs and chanting. One glance and I was glad I'd given in to Angelica's pleas as we stood in the center aisle of J. C. Penney negotiating over which department to turn toward. "What are you trying to look like, a lumberjack or a marine? I'm not about to spend good money on—"

"But it's what everyone's wearing." A response I was particularly sensitive to, my own adolescence having been marked by *otherness.* Angelica argued that clothes are like animal pelts, their textures, colors, and styles identifying the species.

Apparently plaid flannel shirts, jeans, and combat boots identified my daughter as a female adolescent in middle school.

"Save the New River, save the New River," her classmates yelled out. They carried homemade signs on which they'd written in colored markers, *Don't pollute our streams* and *Stop using chemicals.* Angelica bounded out of the car and opened the back door to take out a square of white poster board stapled to a thick wooden strip. *It's our inheritance* was printed in large block letters on the sign.

Foot on the clutch, intending to head over to Piggly Wiggly, I shifted into first gear. I pulled away from the curb.

While the car idled at the next red light, images flashed before me. The shed where Wendell stored dusts and sprays. Ladybugs crawling up my forearm as a lesson to the children that insects are our friends. Angelica holding out bouquets of goldenrod clutched in her tiny fist. Then I saw before me, as vividly as if I stood beside it, the future of the gentle stream running through our farm. Dead fish, starved by a lack of oxygen, floated on top. My eyes flooded with tears.

An impatient honk alerted me that the light had changed to green.

I drove around the block twice, trying to make up my mind. *It's our inheritance.* Wendell considered the farm the kids' inheritance: property without a mortgage, offering a livelihood. Randy would someday cultivate it as Wendell did.

I parked the station wagon, put a quarter in the meter, and walked back to the farm supply store. A few signs were stacked by the curb. I chose "God's creation, ours to protect" and stepped in line behind Angelica.

"Save the New River, save the New River," she was shouting, her voice strong, her jaw set to challenge any who disagreed.

I marched silently, uneasy about being the only adult. I joined the kids, though, because I too saw that Eden was slipping away.

At first I didn't notice Brother Alcorn get out of his Buick across the street and saunter toward the store. A church elder, he wasn't shy about exerting his authority, most recently rebuking Sister Brightwell for campaigning for the Democratic Party when Holy Scripture mandated that we be *in* not *of* the world.

He owned the area's largest apple orchard and ran a big fruit stand over on Route 11. He'd turned himself into a local celebrity by appearing in his own TV ad, singing a jingle, "Young Fred Alcorn had a farm. E-I-E-I-O."

Wearing stylish western jeans and a pale blue dress shirt, ironed creases on the sleeves, he stepped onto the sidewalk. As if expecting the teenagers to recognize and pay homage to him as a local celebrity, he planted his polished loafers a shoulders' width apart and gave the kids an appraising look. His eyes came to rest on me. I stopped in my tracks. Stepping over to me he bellowed, "Sister Elizabeth, does your husband know what you're doing?"

By late afternoon he did.

Angelica was setting the table, I was stirring the gravy. Wendell, without bothering to wipe the manure off his boots, stormed into the kitchen. Not usually one to explode in anger, he was as livid as I'd ever seen him. He pulled two chairs from the kitchen table. "You I'll deal with later," he told me, signaling with a nod of the head that I was to sit. I decided not to argue—not for now. But he wasn't going to like lumpy gravy.

He motioned for Angelica to take the other chair. "Just what do you have to say for yourself, young lady?" He peered down at her, pointing his index finger as he spoke. "So I'm a polluter of streams. Me and all our neighbors here. Please tell me what you've got against the way I earn a living, the means by which you have clothes on your back, food to eat. An explanation, that's what I want."

Angelica stood up, too short by almost a foot to look him in the eyes, but by the changed position lessening the distance between their faces. "Well, you—all those pesticides and herbicides you dump on the fields. And all that manure in the barnyard. Where does it all go when it rains? Into our little stream. Which flows into the New River, which flows into the Ohio, which flows into—"

"Don't go giving me a geography lesson. I won't have you embarrassing me in front of the whole community."

She stepped closer. "Daddy, I didn't mean to embarrass you. I just want people—you in particular—I want y'all to start asking questions. Like how long is Earth going to survive if we keep treating it this way, with so many chemicals and all?" She wrapped her arms around his waist, her intense hazel eyes turned upward, searching his face.

Like the spoonful of butter that minutes earlier had melted in my gravy skillet, his anger dissolved. His shoulders dropped and he held Angelica to him, this man in bib overalls whose barnyard stench overpowered the roast in the oven.

Nevertheless he grounded her for a month, wouldn't even let her go on a band trip to the Apple Harvest Festival.

After Wendell excused Angelica, sending her upstairs, he planted his body in front of my chair. I tried Angelica's tactic. I stood. But we were almost the same height, and I outweighed him by nearly thirty pounds. So instead of disarming him, my move seemed threatening. He took a step back, then reconsidering, came forward to stand eye to eye.

"A girl," he said, "I can see how she—I can make an allowance for her not yet fully understanding the scriptures. But you. It's like you deliberately dishonored me."

I lifted my chin. "I believe we have a responsibility to protect creation."

"God gave man dominion over the earth. That includes beef and chickens and corn and everything else we grow here."

Without thinking, I blurted, "And me?"

Where did that question come from? My whole life I'd been programmed to challenge neither father nor husband.

Wendell shifted his eyes, nervously wet his lips. He inhaled deeply. "Well, uh..."

"Hate to tell you this, Wendell dear, but God has not given you dominion over me."

He stomped away.

I returned to the stove, my hand shaking as I picked up the spoon to check the condition of the gravy. It was scorched.

News of my challenging the very foundation of our local economy—and equally, if not more disgraceful, my husband's means of providing for the family—quickly became the talk of the church. It was as if I'd committed First Woman's sin all over again. The Sisters and Brothers wouldn't have been satisfied merely to condemn Eve's action. They would have donned fake smiles and said hello when their hearts weren't friendly at all.

They would have whispered behind Eve's back and made remarks like, "The fruit must be good this time of year." Finally she would have considered exile a relief.

# A Vision

*The Lord is my shepherd, I shall not want. The Lord is my shepherd, I shall not want... Firecrackers exploding, bonfires burning, guns shot into the air. The Yankees celebrate victory. Yet there is no righteousness in their defeating a just cause. Their victory leaves Southern farmers with land but no one to work it, and Negroes are now without the security of having someone to take care of them. I have heard of the resulting chaos. Through the outside revelry Wilkes and I sit in private parley before the fireplace in my room. Inside can be heard the tick of the clock and the creak of my rocking chair as it shifts my weight from one floorboard to another. "It is futile," I say. "Only a short while until every Southern soldier surrenders." For a spell we remain silent. "If Lincoln were dead..." he says. Unsure of his sincerity I study his profile as he stares into the fire. "His death might bring renewed hope to our people," I say after a time. Wilkes leans forward in his chair. He is a handsome young man, with a wide forehead, well trimmed mustache, and penetrating eyes. Even when he speaks softly, he articulates as if on stage, and uses his hands for dramatic effect. From the corner the clock's steady tick keeps cadence with our words. "He would see the South bow down in defeat," I say. The thought so enrages me that I grasp the wooden arms of the rocking chair with greater firmness. "I am ready to die for the cause," he says. "Are you?" Since the infancy of our kidnapping plan, I too have given the question consideration. If our land is to be saved someone must take more drastic action. Elizabeth. Elizabeth. If our land is to be saved, someone must take drastic action. If our land is to be saved. If our land is to be saved. The Lord is my shepherd. The Lord...*

# Chapter 3



AT THE ENTRANCE of the convent breakfast area, she pauses in front of a Mary figurine atop a credenza. Tiny white electric lights form a halo around her head, a blue rosary hangs from her alabaster fingers.

A memory from years ago. The Holy Name Gift Shop, where Elizabeth went with her only friend, Kathy, a Catholic girl knowledgeable about all things religious, including virginity and the sinfulness of doing *it*. The purchase of a similar figurine, with pensive eyes, along with a pine-scented candle, Mary's picture painted on it.

*Why, Daddy? Why'd you come barging in my room when I was praying to her and shout that I was blaspheming God? You grabbed her out of my hands and threw her down. I stood there, struck dumb as I watched pieces of her body scatter across my bedroom floor. Her body broken for me.*

A vigorous shake of the head brings Elizabeth back to the present.

She gazes around the room, searching for a table. Wide shuttered windows run the length of a wall. They are open, letting in a gentle breeze and sweet floral scents from the courtyard garden below. The faint clamor of Via Barberini echoes in the background. There's noise inside too, all the tables occupied by people speaking different languages.

Two elderly nuns, managing multitudinous yards of black fabric, hobble around, unceremoniously tossing baskets of rolls and narrow chrome racks with butter and jam on each table. Elizabeth watches their laborious shuffling as they try not to spill cappuccino.

Her intent is to ease their workload. But at the serving station at the back of the room, as she pours coffee into a cup, one of the nuns miraculously picks up enough speed to stand before her and scowl. The words coming from the sister's mouth bear no resemblance to the soothing syllables of Italian love songs.

"Scusi, scusi," Elizabeth mutters, putting down the carafe and backing away.

She returns to her table, takes a roll from the basket, and spreads butter on it. Within an hour she'll be stopping for focaccia, maybe indulge in gelato.

She glances up to see an older man about to exit the room. He has a large frame, strands of graying hair combed over a bald spot. Acne scars are embedded in his cheeks. He adjusts his wire-rimmed glasses.

She's swallowing and gasping at the same time. Coffee spurts from her mouth, some landing back in the cup, some spattering on the table.

He looks exactly like her father. Her dead father.

"BUONGIORNO," THE DOORMAN SAYS with a slight bow. He winks. Either he's flirting or something's irritating his eye. Maybe he's signaling that he's on to her charade, that she bears no resemblance to the wealthy women staying at the hotel. In any case she feels the pink rush to her cheeks.

It's early, so there's little activity in the lobby. The concierge is drawing lines on a map for a young couple who, judging from how often they smile into each other's eyes, are newlyweds. She breezes past two desk clerks punching computer keys.

The lounge near the elevators is unoccupied, the TV tuned to CNN. Something about tree sitters in the rainforest of Brazil. She turns up the volume and takes a seat on the plush leather sofa. Why, a person could get dizzy just following the camera's view up to the canopy, which must be as high as a five or six-story building.

She stands and steps closer to the TV. The camera crew can't get a clear view through the thick branches, so neither can she.

*Please, please, don't let Angelica be up there.*

A spokesman for the tree sitters, a young man identified only as Birdman, lowers himself to visibility. He's articulate, speaking of how the world's demand for wood products and more agricultural land leads to the destruction of rainforests. "When you cut down these trees, the carbon they've been storing is released into the atmosphere as carbon dioxide," he tells reporters on the ground. "The emissions contribute to global warming. We're here to protect the planet."

But the reporter's smirk and mocking tone suggest that those up in the heights are over-zealous kooks.

Elizabeth can't help herself. "It's about habitat too." She's speaking to the TV. "The loss of it, that's what's wrong with destroying rainforests." Her voice becomes louder. "The three-toed sloth—how can you not care that the poor creature's endangered? Cut down these trees and it has nowhere safe to live."

Standing no more than three feet from the TV, she talks to it with the forcefulness of a mother insisting on her children's attention. "Those people up in the tree show a lot more courage than you guys who stand down on the ground judging them."

The hotel manager has noticed her: a woman in an ankle-length Guatemalan dress and wide-brimmed straw hat loudly addressing the TV in English. He approaches, eyes glaring. He knows she's not a guest, he says, teeth clenched. She's to leave and not come back. Ever.

Well, she'll just find another hotel.

To: wl83@torbox3.onion          Sept 22  8:03 PM
Subject: hi
Dear One,

I wish you'd given me more specifics. I don't know if your actions are likely to draw local or international attention. In case the answer is international, I plan to check CNN every day. Of course, I fear seeing your face and hearing news that your group has been arrested, or worse.

I remember the terrariums you used to make and the time you built Randy a unicycle for his birthday. How he loved that. You are such a gifted person. You could be anything you set your mind to. Instead you're somewhere—I have no idea where—planning destruction. I know you don't see it that way, but the law will.

Most mothers have dreams about their child's future. I want yours to be filled with laughter and love. Instead you've got this save-the-world notion that can only have a grim outcome. If you want to rescue the planet go finish your studies. Use your knowledge.

I mentioned love. I'm not suggesting marriage is the solution to everything. Heaven knows it didn't work for me. Not for a lot of women. But if you find a man who makes you happy, who fills your days with delight and your nights with passion, go for it.

About my own current situation. Today I begin my search. Given her attitude of late, I'm thinking Mary needs a quiet place where she can collect her thoughts and regain her stamina. She once admitted that she likes admiration as much as mortals. So I'll start with churches.

I love you. Please be careful.
Mom

ELIZABETH GAZES UP into sorrowful eyes. From Mary's arm of marble hang strands of rosaries and a ceramic plaque with "Remember Claudia" painted on it. Pictures of children, stuffed animals, letters of supplication—some yellowed by age—are clustered around her feet.

The vast nave echoes with a father sobbing, *no, no.* A faint whimper hangs in the air, a mother's weeping, without words. Whispered prayers surround Elizabeth. Even though she doesn't speak the language, she recognizes that mothers and fathers are remembering a child, one with dreams of becoming an opera star. A doctor. A painter. Dreamed of…dreamed of…dreamed of. These parents trust that Mary suffers with all mothers and fathers who lose a child to disease, to accident, or violence. That her tears mingle with theirs, that she too cried out to God, demanding to know why her child was taken from her. Like them she suffered from sleepless nights and loss of appetite. She had no reason to believe in a resurrection.

Elizabeth tears a piece of paper from her notebook, writes "Remember Angelica," and places it at the statue's feet. "My daughter who is so much like your son," she whispers as she kneels. "Just as head strong. Just as determined to change the world."

"EXCUSE ME, DO you speak English?" A young man stands before her, his shoulders sagging under the weight of a backpack. He wears an earring and his sandy-blond hair hangs below his ears. The skin on his cheeks is pitted. The stubble on his chin is a mixture of light brown and blond hairs. A college student she's guessing. Yet he looks familiar.

"Yes, I speak English."

"I'm lost." There's frustration, a little fear even, in his voice.

In fact, she herself has been walking in circles and only in the past minute or so figured out where she is. She steps closer and points on her map to the corner where they're standing. "Where do you want to be?" she asks.

He's searching for a youth hostel near Campo de'Fiori. She shows him how to get there, still puzzling over how familiar he looks.

"This is my first trip out of the U.S." He seems to relax now that he knows where he is. She responds to his wide grin with a smile of her own, at the same time taking note of wire-rimmed glasses resting crookedly on his nose. "I can hardly wait to see it all. I love history, especially ancient history."

"Where are you from?" she asks, as much from her sense of familiarity as from politeness.

"Florida. Orlando."

Since he's no older than twenty, there's little chance they met there, so she doesn't bother telling him it's where she grew up.

"Oh," is all she says. "Well, I hope Rome's all you've anticipated."

He reaches out to shake her hand. "My name's Vernon. Thanks so much for your help."

He flashes the most beguiling of grins as they both nod goodbye, he heading in one direction, she in the opposite. She shakes her head in disbelief. Except for the earring and hair hanging over his ears, the young man looks like her father in his high school graduation picture. He even has her father's name.

To: wl83@torbox3.onion                    Sept 23 7:31AM
Subject: hi
Dear One,

Be ye not of this world, Daddy would admonish your Uncle Daniel and me, meaning we were not to do what other kids did, like wear clothes that were in style or dance or play cards. Daddy also believed the scripture means don't get involved. If the world's all messed up, pray about it. Cast your worries on the Lord. God's in charge and we are not to doubt his purposes.

As much as I reject Daddy's theology, I want to say, Angelica, be not of this world. Pray about these things. I want to believe that some higher power is in control, though I admit evidence points to the contrary. Don't lay your life on the line. Jesus already tried that and look what good it did.

Love,
Mom

AS SHE CLICKS *Send,* tears follow her face's shallow furrows, the result of working in the sun, gaining and losing weight over the years.

She glances over to see a teenage girl at a nearby computer looking at her sympathetically. Hair dyed purple, the girl has a nose ring, a griffin tattoo on her upper arm. She's wearing a short black leather skirt with a metal chain belt. What must her mother think of the girl's appearance? Elizabeth wipes the tears away with her forearm and smiles at the girl, who smiles back.

How do other mothers come to accept their daughters' decisions?

# A Vision

*He leadeth me in paths of righteousness for his name sake. He leadeth me in paths of righteousness… "Of course my death is not inevitable," Wilkes says. "Several allies in the countryside will aid me—for I assume I must be the one to carry out the deed. After I cross the river, I shall be in friendly territory." His face shines, his dark eyes glisten, more from his excitement than from the glow of the fire. "Once the Confederacy learns of Lincoln's death, it will gain new courage and determination. The North will be without a leader." In the fireplace a log drops, the coals crackle. "A statue in Richmond, I envision it. The two of us, you and I. The inscription will read, 'When others believed the cause to be lost, they heeded the call.'" I am inspired by his words. I see the statue too. After the independence of the South is secured for all time, Wilkes and I shall be remembered as true patriots who risked our lives on its behalf. Elizabeth, Elizabeth, you must have courage. You must have courage. He leadeth me in paths of righteousness… He leadeth me in the paths…*

# Chapter 4

MATTISON FAMILY LIFE, like that of my childhood, centered around the Community of Brothers, founded in the eighteenth century by Helmut Meisterfeld. A religious sect with its roots going back to Germany, it espouses a lifestyle of separateness, being *in* not *of* the world, though the difference between *in* and *of* has never been clear to me.

In any case, while growing up, I wanted more than anything to be *of* the world. To be normal. Normal girls wore brightly colored clothes, shorts even. They wore a variety of hair styles. Normal girls knew the words to love songs they heard on the radio. Bracelets hung from their arms, necklaces from their necks. Most enviable of all was the fun they had within circles of friendship, whispering secrets, passing notes. I overheard them make plans to attend Saturday afternoon movies and have slumber parties.

Kathy Harmon and I were the only ones not included. Kathy because she wore thick glasses, had crooked teeth, and committed social suicide by constantly demonstrating that she was by far the smartest girl in the class. Me, because I was not *of the world*.

Like my mother and the other Sisters, I wore dresses hand-sewn of cotton, all according to the same pattern: a bibbed bodice to conceal the curvature of the breasts (though as a girl I had nothing to conceal), hemline at mid-calf, three-quarter length sleeves. Women obeyed the Apostle Paul's directive not to cut their hair. Mama braided mine in pigtails or coiled like snakes around my head. I was baptized at the age of ten, which meant I had to wear the prayer covering of white netting all the time, even to school.

Like many sects, the Community of Brothers became less rigid over time. We women made gradual adjustments to our dresses, raising the hem a little, doing away with the front panel that hid the fullness of our breasts, replacing cotton with synthetic fabric. After a while, instead of sewing our clothes, we bought them at J.C. Penney and Sears. Pants became acceptable, most often made of polyester with elastic waist bands, as we tended to be on the hefty side.

I never intended to challenge any of the Brothers' rules. It just sort of happened.

THE CHURCH SANCTUARY was simple, no crosses or velvet drapes in front, no curtains on the windows. No padding on the benches. Only recently had the elders agreed to allow the purchase of a Hammond organ, though so far only Sister Ebersole expressed a willingness to take on the responsibility of accompanying congregational singing. She did all right as long as the hymn had no more than one sharp or one flat.

In the sixth row from the front, I sat beside Wendell, looking up at the pulpit, an unadorned block of shellacked oak, where Brother Baker waved his Bible above his head. Instead of listening carefully, I was imagining him having sex with Sister Winona. Not because I personally found him appealing. Just the opposite. Surely Sister Winona had to turn her head to keep from being distracted by the clusters of broken veins on his nose or by the bushy eyebrows that spanned the width of his face. His breath probably smelled like a garbage dump. Good lord, what must he look like without clothes on? Probably like that dead opossum Angelica found in the backyard.

"'For every woman that prayeth or prophesiath with her head uncovered dishonoreth her head…'" I reached up to make sure my prayer covering was secure atop my braided knot of hair. In recent years an increasing number of gray strands had overtaken the ripe-persimmon color. "'For a man indeed ought not to cover his head, forasmuch as he is the image and glory of God, but the woman is the glory of the man.'" Brother Baker leaned forward, rested his elbow on the pulpit, and pointed his index finger.

"Now there's been dissension among us, some Sisters saying they do not need to wear the prayer covering except in church."

He had my full attention, for indeed there had been a discussion at the last meeting of Ladies' Aid, with Sisters Louise and Eleanor questioning the prayer covering's relevance in modern times. "It's a relic from the past," Sister Eleanor had said.

"I have even seen one of our own," Brother Baker said, "walking about in public bareheaded. But the Apostle Paul says, it's right here in First Corinthians, Brothers and Sisters, that—why must a woman cover her head? Because, Brothers and Sisters, the prayer covering symbolizes to the world—it is a testimony to our neighbors of the attitude God wants a woman to have."

Having been part of the Community of Brothers since birth, I knew what attitude he was referring to. I sat straight and turned an ear toward him. I wanted to be sure I heard his explanation correctly.

"Man is the image and glory of God, while the woman—she wears the covering to show—it's a sign she knows she was created for the glory of the man. And she doesn't keep this spirit of humility just on Sunday mornings, Sisters and Brothers. She accepts her subordination to her husband the whole week long. In her home, in the church, and in town."

I had noticed the way Sister Winona let him grab her wrist and pull her along, how quiet she was in his presence. Yet she had no reason to be subordinate to that little—that opossum posing as a man. She was an intelligent woman who graduated summa cum laude from Meisterfeld College and had been offered a scholarship into a master's program at Princeton. But her mother warned her she'd never find a man willing to marry her if she went. "Men feel threatened by smart women," Sister Winona had more than once said with confidence at Ladies' Aid.

Several years ago, when there'd been talk on TV about women's lib, Wendell had said, "I'm sure glad you're not into any of that stuff." I assured him I was quite satisfied with my role.

But that's what had been eating at me lately, a suspicion that I wasn't really satisfied.

After church, shuffling between kitchen and dining room, I placed a platter of pork tenderloin and new potatoes in front of

Wendell and Randy. A casserole of squash, eggs, and cheese next to Angelica. (After witnessing the butchering of chickens at a young age, she'd declared herself a vegetarian. Not surprisingly, her stance continued to irritate Wendell, producer of beef cattle, keeper of five hogs and twenty laying hens, with fryers in the freezer).

"I don't get it," Angelica said as soon as Wendell finished thanking God for the food and the hands that prepared it. Her words were directed at me. "You wear a prayer covering because—something to do with…? You believe God wants you to do everything Daddy says because he's made more in the image of God than you are. And your main purpose in life is to make Daddy look good, but his is to make God look good. Is that right?"

"That's right," Wendell said.

"What if Mom's smarter than you are? I'm not saying one of you is smarter than the other. But what if she was?"

"Your mother and I, we divide the responsibilities. It's her job to manage the house and my—"

"According to Brother Baker, your job is to pretty much manage her and everything else."

"Well, if you want to look at it that way. I can assure you, men carry a heavy responsibility."

"And Mom doesn't?"

"Not as much as a man."

Randy, whose attention had been focused on the chicken breast he ate with his fingers, set it down on the plate. He licked his fingers one by one, looked at his younger sister with a leer. "Yeah, not as much as a man."

Out in the driveway a horn honked. In two big bites Randy finished his mashed potatoes and pushed his chair from the table.

"May I please be excused?" I suggested in a tone of motherly correction.

"Uh, may I please be excused." Not a question. He rushed from the dining room. Metal hangers clanged in the hall closet as he grabbed a jacket. The front door slammed.

Later, while Angelica did homework at the kitchen table and Wendell stretched out on the sofa alternating between napping and watching a baseball game on TV, I sat in front of the window of my sewing alcove. I peered out across the valley without focusing my gaze on anything. What did accepting my subservience to Wendell say to Angelica, a girl possibly as intelligent as Sister Winona?

Wear the prayer covering so you'll be like me? Wear it so you'll someday be able to find a husband? Wear it so if you're more capable than your husband, you'll know your place and not use your intellect?

What did it say to Randy, who since childhood had imitated Wendell? As a little boy he'd pushed a toy wheelbarrow, taking running steps to keep up with his daddy. Spent hours in the field, perched on Wendell's lap on the seat of the John Deere tractor.

I reached up to remove the bobby pins holding the cap of white netting atop my knot of uncut hair. I carefully folded the prayer covering and placed it in my sewing box.

"Put it on," Wendell later demanded. I ignored him, going about my household chores as usual. For several nights, as I lay beside him in bed, he dropped his authoritarian tone and pleaded, adding *please*. "Please don't make such a big deal of this." "Please don't embarrass me this way." "It's just a little cap made of that…whatever that flimsy stuff is. Please."

"I'm thinking of Angelica. To you it's just a little cap of netting. I don't want her thinking she's supposed to—supposed to crush all that intellect and creativity." I'd roll onto my side, my back to him. End of discussion.

I TOSSED MY APRON over the back of a kitchen chair and rushed out the front door. As usual, I was late. In preparation for Sunday dinner, I'd peeled potatoes, now soaking in cold water, prepared meatloaf, and set the oven timer to turn on during church. Angelica's beans and rice casserole needed only to be heated.

It felt like an ambush. Wendell stood just outside the door. His hands grasped both of my arms. His eyes scanned the top of my head. "Aren't you even going to put it on for church?"

"No."

"Get in the car," he ordered Angelica, who waited on the flagstone walkway in a skirt challenging her father's length requirements. She looked at me questioningly then slid into the backseat. Though Randy was already behind the wheel, Wendell signaled with a nod of the head his intention to drive.

I remained on the porch, arms crossed in defiance. Wendell slammed the car door shut, revved the engine, and headed down the long driveway, gravel flying.

Maybe he'd turn around. The family that prays together… No, he'd not apologize; well, neither would I. I didn't leave my stance but kept my feet firmly planted, waiting for an idea of what to do next. The pointed ends of my new beige shoes scrunched my toes. My new purse felt heavy on my forearm. My pantyhose pinched my crotch. I slipped off my shoes, set the purse down, and pulled off the pantyhose.

I sat down on the porch swing and with bare toes pushed myself back and forth. I inhaled the spring air drifting across the wide valley. Nearby a pair of wrens answered each other's mating song. The graceful blossoms of the nearby dogwood reminded me of Japanese prints I'd recently admired in an art catalog obviously mailed by mistake. I'd spent more than fifteen minutes turning its pages. The nearest art museum of any size was in Washington. If I left now I could make the trip and be home by evening. By midnight at the latest.

Back and forth. The rhythmic squeaking of the swing's chain. Back and forth. The art museum. The sweet scent of spring air. Squeak. Squeak.

*I've been taught to stand up for what I believe.* More than a year earlier Angelica had risked Wendell's anger and that of every farmer in the community. *I've been taught to stand up for what I believe.* I went back in the house for a key to the pickup truck.

While worshippers sang "Stand up, stand up for Jesus," my ample frame sashayed down the center aisle and stood next to Wendell on the sixth row. I did not wear a prayer covering. Nor did I wear pantyhose. I had on sneakers.

~~~
~~~

"WHAT BROUGHT YOU AND DADDY TOGETHER?" Angelica once asked. Soon after the prayer covering fiasco, as I recall. "You're so different."

Social ineptitude, I was tempted to say, but didn't. Wendell's from being raised fatherless and given the responsibilities of running the farm at an early age. Mine from growing up in a cheerless, authoritarian household. The absence of a father in Wendell's case, the presence of one in mine.

Neither would I share many memories of college.

So I didn't tell her that as a freshman I'd arrived at Meisterfeld College, one of a handful of girls who still wore the prayer covering and cotton dresses well below the knee. Others wore clothes *of the world*: body-hugging skirts, sweaters molded to the breasts, and casual pants (though they weren't allowed in class). These same girls promenaded along campus sidewalks holding the hand of a boy or laughing with a roommate. I had no boyfriend and my roommate, Yoshiko, a Japanese girl with limited English, spent most of her time with two other students from Japan.

I was shy, hesitant to reach out. Angelica would be shocked to know how sex and alcohol offered me entry into a circle of—I can hardly use the word *friends*. I was a girl desperate for acceptance. And, having grown up in a cheerless household, desperate for fun. I wanted to laugh as I saw others laugh, with belly guffaws. I was accepted by a small group who weren't the kind to run for class office or lead prayer in chapel. Two boys were expelled in an off-campus sting at a nearby bar. Twice I was threatened with expulsion: once when I was caught sneaking a smoke behind the library; the other time when the night watchman shined his flashlight on me, out of the dorm after curfew. With a boy. During that period, which included most of my freshman year, I borrowed clothes from another girl and quit wearing my prayer covering.

"I met your father during the first chapel of my sophomore year," I told her. "When the preacher offered the invitation."

"You went forward?"

"That's right."

At the base of the podium, while students sang, "Just as I am, without one plea," the chapel speaker had stood, arms extended as if embracing everyone in the auditorium. "Oh, children of God, don't flee his open arms. The world lures us with its false promises of freedom. But true freedom can only be found in the arms of Jesus."

Being *of the world* wasn't turning out to be all that great. I was still lonely. I wanted somebody, maybe Jesus, to put his arms around me, say *I love you.* Tears streaming down my cheeks, I pushed past the other students standing in the pew. "O, Lamb of God, I come," they sang as they stepped back to allow me through.

No, I didn't mention the depth of my loneliness.

"I'd strayed," I told Angelica.

"What do you mean, strayed?" Full of questions, that girl.

"I don't want to go into detail, Honey. So during the same hymn, here I am making my way out of the pew. Pow! I bump into this cute guy named Wendell Mattison coming out on the other side of the aisle. I guess we both had our heads lowered and weren't looking where we were going. We bumped heads, nearly knocked each other down." Angelica and I shared a faint laugh. "When we finally got our bearings, he took my arm, and we walked forward arm in arm."

"Aw, that was sweet."

"Yes, I guess it was. Afterwards he invited me to the snack shop for a cup of coffee."

"But what—I guess I want to know *why,* why you got married. What did you see in each other?"

"I can only speak for myself. Like I said, he was cute. And he was a serious young man, a senior accounting major. I knew he'd be a good provider."

Why? By marrying Wendell I found comfort in renewed ties with the church. I understood its ethos. I accepted its rules.

Until I didn't.


I DROVE INTO TOWN to buy diet pills I'd seen advertised on TV, and canning jar lids for the strawberry jam I planned to make. The only available parking spaces were a block off the main street, in front of some of the fine old homes: frame structures with wide front porches and, in a few cases, additions the size of the original house. Lawns were manicured, hedges neatly trimmed. A jocko lawn statue holding a lantern stood by the steps of the house I parked in front of.

Purchases made, I was returning to the car when I came upon a hopscotch court drawn with pink chalk on the sidewalk. Turning to make sure no one watched, I rested purse and packages against the trunk of a maple tree. Something to mark the square, that's what I needed, some gently sliding object similar to the short chain I used to toss as a girl. Mark the square to remind myself and other players where I was, mark my progress from beginning to end. The chain attached to my change purse would do.

Far less nimbly than when I was a girl of eight or nine, I hopped blocks one, two, and three. Feet apart for four and five, hop on six, feet apart for seven and eight, hop on nine, turn around on the same foot and return to where I started. Toss the marker to two, then to three.

No one was there to tell me I stepped on a line. That's what the argument had been about in fourth grade, out on the black macadam of the school playground, when the teacher forced a group of girls to include Kathy Harmon and me. "Yes you did," one of the girls said firmly. "No I didn't," another insisted. "Look at Elizabeth," someone said. "She's the farthest behind and she doesn't argue every time we catch her stepping on the line."

My life until now. Never complaining. Forever trying to keep other people happy. Daddy, Wendell, the kids.

Across the street a woman pulled back organdy curtains. Gave me a cold stare. Clumsily I reached down for my marker, stepped over to the tree, picked up purse and packages, and headed for the car.

*Why did I stop to play hopscotch?* I asked myself as I drove home. *Something to do with stepping on lines. Over the lines. Lines intended for separation, clarity. This kind of behavior belongs on one side, that kind on the other. Is that why little girls play hopscotch, so we'll learn not to step over the lines?*

*It's my law, Father God decreed. It's the way we do things, the church says. Stay in the box we have drawn. But what if the draw-er of the lines has made some squares too small or placed them according to his whim*—and I deliberately chose to think "his." *What if the lines become a prison? Am I supposed to accept it? Work to stay in it without teetering or falling just because someone arbitrarily drew the line?*

ON THE EVENING of the Big Confrontation, I sat at the kitchen table in front of the Scrabble board, competing with myself. I'd just put down *toxic,* the x landing on "triple letter score."

A voice as squeaky as an ungreased gate hinge came from the living room: "Elizabeth, come here, we need to talk."

I recorded my thirty-four points. As I passed the kitchen counter I reached for a dishtowel. Like a child's security blanket, a towel in hand offered comfort, something to cling to during a stressful moment. Wendell wasn't the kind of man to discuss his feelings. So I knew his "we need to talk" implied serious business. Serious business meant stress for me.

He motioned for me to sit on the sofa, taking for himself the recliner in front of the TV.

He leaned back in the chair, fingers gripping the armrests. Six times he cleared his throat. "Elder Spitzer," he finally said, "pulled me aside after church. He said the elders discussed all the trouble you're making."

*All* the trouble. No sooner had I stopped wearing a prayer covering than several other women did too, Sister Winona among them. Now I suspected that the Court of Brotherly Opinion was considering another transgression: my bringing up a forbidden topic with the Sisters.

The newspaper had recently covered a story about the escape of a fifteen-year-old girl imprisoned for two years in a basement, where she'd been repeatedly raped. Over ham sandwiches at the monthly Ladies' Aid, I had asked, "If God is all powerful, how could he let such a horrible thing happen?" Which, I later learned, led some Sisters to ask the same question of their husbands.

"Wendell, no one's answered my question." I rolled up the dishtowel, twisting it into the shape of a pretzel, at the same time peering pleadingly into his eyes. It had never been my intent to cause trouble.

"God is in charge and he has his reasons, which we are not to question."

"If God loves that girl and he's all powerful, he would not have let that happen."

"Elizabeth, I'm telling you to keep these thoughts to yourself. Bringing them out in the open, it—it disrupts the fellowship. The prayer covering business is already an embarrassment to the family. Think of the kids. Think of me."

I unfolded the dishtowel and spread it out flat on my lap. I gazed down at my hands, clasped in the center. "So what am I supposed to do," I asked, a hint of sarcasm in my voice, "ponder these things in my heart?" I looked up. "If God can't handle my questions…"

"Brother Spitzer just said I'm supposed to tell you to stop." Poor Wendell, I thought, watching his adam's apple shift as he took a deep swallow. A spineless man whose authority lay in the Brothers' interpretation of scripture.

No, not poor Wendell. I jumped from the sofa and shook my index finger at him, so startling him that his whole body jerked back and a gasp escaped his throat.

"And you didn't defend me. You didn't say, 'I've been wondering the same thing.' If Brother Spitzer said I'm not to question authority, then all you have to do is tell me to shut up and that will be it. Is that what you thought, Wendell?"

His eyes watered; the jaw beneath his five-o'clock-shadow quivered. "Well…a…well, I assumed we'd talk about it, and you'd see my point, and you'd…this time you'll listen to me…won't you?"

I continued to stand before him, feet spread defiantly. "And exactly what is your point? You've told me Brother Spitzer's but you haven't said anything about *your point.*"

"All I want is harmony. In the church and at home."

"Harmony. If I wear a prayer covering and don't ask questions about the Almighty, then we'll all get along fine." I turned toward the kitchen. "Well fuck the Brothers!"

I came to an abrupt stop, as shocked as he was by what had just escaped my mouth. A word from when I'd hung out with college misfits. Wendell leaped to his feet. "I'll have no profanity in my house."

I came back and stood so that we were nose to nose. "In *your house?*"

"I-I-I mean in our house."

When making strawberry jam, the cook skims off foam that's come to the top of the boiling mixture. Like the foam, anger had been rising inside me. I had no idea how to skim it off. Or if I even wanted to.

AT THE NEXT MEETING of Ladies' Aid I asked why couldn't God be Mother and not just Father, like when Jesus referred to God as a mother hen. Which led the Sisters to wonder too and pass the question on to their husbands. In August the Brothers called a special meeting, where they officially ordered me to cease disrupting the fellowship.

The planet was shifting. Jarring my world. Leaving my dizzy. Wobbly.

# A Vision

*Thou anointest my head with oil. Thou anointest my… In John's tavern he sits with his friends, in their drunkenness slurring words of condemnation against the Northern states. I step into the room, not disagreeing but with the desire to speak my own mind. I say it is unfair for the stronger to enforce its will upon the weaker, that the North pressures us to sacrifice while it relinquishes nothing that is central to its way of life. The time has come for the South to take a stand against tyranny. I'm better educated than the lot of them, yet John condemns my speaking. What will become of the South is up to its men, he says, not its women. Sometimes, Elizabeth, you must leave the fools to their own idiocy. Thou anointest my head with oil. Thou anointest…*

# Chapter 5

A RUFFLED APRON protected my mauve cotton dress. Shaped like a pyramid, the dress no doubt accentuated my wide hips. In spite of my efforts to be on time, the pies I'd made for the after-church potluck dinner still baked in the oven.

"Angelica," I called out, "put down your book and finish getting ready."

"Randy, did you find your belt?" At the end of the summer he would head to Virginia Tech for the fall semester of his freshman year. "What's your father doing?"

"He's out in the car waiting," Randy said.

"Wendell," I yelled out the door, "The pies need ten more minutes. Why don't you go ahead and take the kids? I'll go over in the truck as soon as I can."

"Let me drive you," Angelica pleaded. She'd been driving a tractor since her feet could reach the pedals and at fourteen thought she qualified as family chauffeur.

"No, it's against the law. Besides, you know your father doesn't like you to be late for Sunday school."

"Aw, Mom." She let the screen door slam behind her.

Twenty minutes later I drove down the gravel driveway. Two hot apple pies wrapped in kitchen towels rested on the floor of the Chevy pickup. It was a beautiful day, the sky a sapphire blue. I opened the window, inhaling the aroma of Jon Brickman's second cutting of hay, not caring that the wind loosened strands of my hair.

At the corner beyond the cemetery—final resting place of Wendell's forebears—the main road intersected the narrow winding one leading to the church. I put my foot on the brake and came to a stop. Looked to the right, in the direction of the church. To the left. To the right again.

I gunned the accelerator. I drove straight ahead. Sped by the used farm equipment lot, the Chevrolet dealer, and Peterson's Auto Parts. On out Eastern Pike, through town and beyond, my thoughts scrambled like a word jumble. Fields of upright corn stalks, patches of woods, cross roads leading to neighboring towns—I passed them all.

Fifty-five, the speed limit. I headed south on Route 11 driving 70. Reveling in my freedom to go faster, slow down, turn at any crossroads, or change direction and go home. My choice. Toward the Tennessee border the valley widened. Phalanxes of low wispy clouds cast mottled shadows on hills far to my right.

I glanced at the gas gauge. The dial jiggled on E. Well, if I ran out of gas, I'd walk. Maybe even hitchhike. Now wouldn't that be something? A fifty-seven-year-old woman, wearing Sunday clothes, standing on the shoulder of the road waving her thumb at passing cars. As I laughed out loud at the very thought, a filling station came into view.

A young man about Randy's age stood behind the counter. Cartons of cigarettes lined the wall behind him. Chrome racks of candies and snack foods formed a barrier between him and customers.

"Add a pack of Marlboros," I said on impulse, handing over my credit card. "And here—a Twinkie. Is there a park, a picnic area somewhere nearby?" I pictured myself strolling around a pond, eating the Twinkie and smoking a cigarette. Absorbing the beauty of the day.

"Next light turn left. It's just a few blocks."

But there was no pond. I parked between two yellow lines and turned off the engine. In front of me, among clusters of wood tables, picnickers gathered. Inside the truck I lit a cigarette. Inhaled deeply. I anticipated the clamor rattling around in my brain to go away, bring some calmness. Instead a spasm of coughing sent my head pitching forward. It hit the steering wheel, and I couldn't tell which was worse, the pain in my chest or my throbbing forehead. Smoking wasn't the pleasure I remembered from my foray into college rebellion.

Massaging my forehead, I studied a group congregating under a pavilion. Two men carried picnic baskets to a chain of tables then slapped each other on the back in greeting. Two women embraced before opening the baskets. Children welcomed each other with squeals of excitement. When an older couple arrived, the children skipped to meet them.

A reminder of family. Clearly I'd failed mine, becoming more an embarrassment than the nurturer a woman is supposed to be. As a young girl I'd put the brakes on the incessant questions and observations that crowded my brain. Why couldn't I do it now? Why couldn't I just make myself fit in with the Sisters and Brothers?

Poor Wendell. No longer in charge of his wife, as a man was supposed to be.

What God hath joined together… How could anyone think God created our union? As a twenty-year-old I simply lacked options. Return home to live with a meek mother and a depressed father, an intimidating man whose control I couldn't stand up to. Or meander through college friendless and disinterested in my studies.

What God hath joined together… Maybe God was responsible for the mess my life was in. And it was a mess. I'd been trying to please God, please Daddy, please the Brothers for so long that goodness had turned sour, like the taste in your mouth after you've vomited. I figured I'd been vomiting a long time and not telling anybody, not even myself, how terrible life tasted.

No, the vile taste in my mouth was from the cigarette. I crushed it in the ash tray, started the engine, and put the truck in reverse. I again headed south on Route 11.

By now Wendell was no doubt wondering what had happened to me. The potluck dinner would be underway, the Sisters displaying their culinary masterpieces atop plastic red and white checkered tablecloths. Meatloaf, fried chicken, green bean casserole, escalloped potatoes. And desserts. My how the Brothers loved pies and cakes, devouring them so quickly that by the time we Sisters had our turn at the dessert table nothing remained but the cookies Anna Herschberger bought at the day-old bakery.

Ahead Holstein cows stood in the shade of a broad oak tree beside a wide gravel shoulder. I pulled over and shut off the engine. Unwrapped the Twinkie, but set it back on the seat, deciding that this time I'd get to my apple pie before the Brothers did.

Standing next to the fence, I drew the glass pie plate to my chin, pushed the palm of my hand beneath the bottom crust, and broke off a large chunk. Usually proud of my flaky crusts and the consistency of my pies, I took notice of neither as I scooped and chewed, scooped and chewed. The cows looked at me with bored stares. Their tails swatted at pesky flies. When the whole pie was gone, I wiped my sticky hands on my dress and got back in the truck.

Near Bristol I abandoned the smooth pavement of Route 11 for a winding rural road. *Welcome to Tennessee,* a sign said. Awhile later, *Welcome to North Carolina.*

The road ran between two mountain ridges, following a river flowing unhurriedly where it was wide; in narrower places, sweeping frantically around boulders. I passed a whitewater rafting business, a sawmill. The temperature was cooler here than at—I started to think *at home,* then decided against it. Not because I'd given thought to returning or not returning, but because the word inferred a place of belonging, and right now I didn't belong on the Virginia farm or among the Sisters and Brothers. I'd never belonged anywhere.

I shifted into second gear as the pickup truck climbed, slowly and laboriously wending its way through a narrow gap. Up a steep incline to my left, the deep green of firs contrasted with the summer-faded green of deciduous trees. Briefly I lost sight of the river, until in front of me, as the road curved to the right, a meager waterfall trickled over a low ledge. I had but a moment to wonder what happened to the river before I had to maneuver a series of descending s-curves.

I was about to increase my speed on a stretch of straight road bisecting a narrow valley, when a sprawling frame farmhouse, its foundation of river rock, came into view. The house appeared unloved and uncared for, with a sagging front porch and a yard of thigh-high weeds. A *For Sale* sign by the road was all the invitation I needed to pull into the gravel driveway.

An expanse of overgrown grass sloped gently down to a pond. A barn of gray weathered boards leaned at such a pitch that a slight push of the hand seemed capable of knocking it over. A rusted barbed-wire fence marked the boundary of the barnyard and a neglected apple orchard. Beyond the barn and orchard lay uncultivated rolling fields leading up to forest-covered mountains.

I pictured myself seated in a lawn chair on a patio shaded by a grape arbor. The grass leading down to the pond, mowed; the long-neglected apple orchard, weeded and pruned, white springtime blossoms sprinkling the branches.

Entangled in these images of possibility, I got out of the truck to follow the narrow brick sidewalk leading to the house. I pressed my face against the picture window. Torn yellowed shades at the other windows kept the room in partial darkness. Barely visible was a stone fireplace at the end of the room, a stairway to its left.

From the house I made my way down the slope toward the pond. Burrs clung to my sticky dress, sharp sticks tore at my pantyhose. At the pond's edge, beside a spreading willow tree with yellowing leaf tips, I squatted to run my fingers through the water. Cool to the touch, it sent calming rays up my arm and across my shoulders. I scooped up a bowl of water with both hands, splashed it on my face. And laughed. Not the laugh of a crazed mind, which some might argue possessed me, but one of simple pleasure.

I returned to a standing position, feet planted apart, my gaze taking in the mountains guarding this swath of valley. In the distance a hawk caught an updraft then dove for prey beyond my vision. Nearby a crow cawed, *let me out, let me out!*

An extraordinary sensation came over me. As if gravity were exerting its full strength, it grasped my ankles. Pulled them toward Earth's core. Deeper, deeper. Until my legs were entwined with the willow tree's roots. Unable to take even one step, I could only put hands to my face and sob. Not out of helplessness or loneliness, but from the overwhelming feeling of connection. To Earth and to this particular spot on the planet.

LATER ANGELICA WOULD TELL ME about the reaction back in Virginia.

Wendell, seated alone in church, didn't know what to make of my tardiness. He was even more perplexed when I didn't show up for the covered dish dinner. All the same he made an excuse for me: I wasn't feeling well. Yes, he'd pass on the Sisters' concern. Upon returning home and finding the pickup gone, he spent the afternoon driving around looking for me.

Monday evening I phoned to say I was safe but not coming back. Wendell went silent, Randy cursed, Angelica cried.

In the weeks that followed, one of the Brothers frequently stopped by in the evening. Wendell would call Randy and Angelica downstairs. The Brothers no doubt thought they were helping, asking the family to kneel on the living room carpet and pray that I would see the error of my ways and return. But they knew, Wendell, Randy, and Angelica, that no amount of prayer was going to bring me back.

# A Vision

*Secede from the union, Elizabeth. Secede from the union.*

# Chapter 6

**ROME**

CONFIDENCE. THAT'S WHAT IT TAKES to be a successful impostor. Walk in like you belong. Though Elizabeth learned her lesson at the other hotel: don't draw attention to yourself.

The man standing behind the tall ledge of the reception desk is distracted. It's clear, judging from his loud, authoritative voice, that he's in charge and that the young woman wearing a navy blue suit has done something he considers wrong. She's crying.

Elizabeth walks past them to a lounge just off the lobby. Like a strobe light, the room's monstrous chandelier throws her off-balance. A draft disturbs myriad crystal teardrops hanging from it, causing rainbows of color to dance about. She staggers a moment before turning up the volume on the TV. She takes the nearest seat, an uncomfortable chair upholstered in red velvet, and waits for news she hopes won't appear.

Before long her chin rests on her chest, a faint snore escapes her mouth. *Sabotage.* She jerks to alertness. In Tennessee. Not all that far from home. At a coal-fired power plant. Yesterday someone entered an underground vault and cut cables then fired guns at transformers. Fourteen transformers were damaged, the Tennessee Valley Authority reports. They'll have to shut down the plant for an undetermined length of time. The vandalism has to have been well thought through, authorities claim, not the act of drunken teenagers.

Six, maybe seven, years ago. Has it been that long since Angelica stomped through the house ranting about acid rain? She was working on a science paper and had just interviewed a guy—Chip Something-or-Other, a ranger over at the Smokies.

The worst air quality of any national park, he'd told her. Power plants in Tennessee burn tons of coal every day.

It's the kind of situation that could incite Angelica to take action. Elizabeth finds comfort, though, knowing that her daughter and high-powered guns are incompatible. Or do new recruits get trained in such matters?

IT'S ONLY A FEW BLOCKS to Maria sopra Minerva, described in her Rome guidebook as having been built on the site of a temple to Minerva. Not unthinkable that Mary would seek refuge in the former home of another so-called virgin. The two could yuk it up together, make up Virgin Mary and Virgin Minerva jokes, maybe invite the headless Catherine of Sienna to escape her crypt and join them.

In Rome's churches Elizabeth has been inhaling the fragrance of incense, looking at the bold reds and blues of painted glass windows, listening to echoes of worshippers' and tourists' steps. She's aware of her connection to earlier generations, women in particular, coming here to appeal to Mary for protection. From war, from disease. For their children and husbands. For themselves.

In a side chapel Elizabeth stands before a fresco: Gabriel blessing the Holy Mother-to-be while she herself blesses the cardinal and St. Thomas Aquinas. It's an invitation-only event, and Elizabeth's not on the guest list. She must stay outside the window with the common people, who know something important is going on in there; otherwise why would dignitaries be stopping by?

She recognizes the expression on Mary's face: fear for this child in the womb. A Jewish baby born under the rule of Rome's puppet-king; a black baby born into a racist society; a doe born into a hunters' woodland; an African elephant born where its ivory tusks will be valued more than its life.

Mary's son, when he reaches adulthood, won't dare meet the gaze of a Roman soldier, won't dare look admiringly upon a daughter of the priestly class. He'll be forbidden to preach that the land of their ancestors will only be returned if the people's hearts change. He will, after all, be a Jewish peasant. That's why

Lippi put that expression on Mary's face, the look of feeling blessed but at the same time fearful for her baby's future.

A HANDFUL OF PEOPLE, mostly women, have gathered for mass. Elizabeth sits off to the side, near the back. She closes her eyes, listening to the swelling strains of the pipe organ; opens them to study the priest whose benevolent bearing reminds her of the many Good Shepherds she's seen during recent days. As he speaks, his voice as gentle as his appearance, she understands none of the words. He lifts a silver plate and chalice. Protestants aren't supposed to take communion in a Catholic church, she's heard. Besides, it's a ritual she'd rather avoid, cannibalistic with its *this is my body, this is my blood.* But watching others step into the aisle, she feels compelled to join them.

The wafer melts on her tongue as she returns to her seat, hands clasped in front of her.

*With this cup, with this bread—my body, my blood. Mary's son was executed, and now my daughter is taking a stand that will imperil her life. We lose our children, that's what the bread and cup symbolize. Our sons die trying to save the world; our daughters die—they die, they die—because they are trying to save the world too. Communion draws me into a circle of mothers with headstrong children.*

> To: wl83@torbox3.onion          Sept 25 8:16 AM
> Subject: Hello
> Dear One,
>
> When you told me you were thinking about dropping out of graduate school, all I could do was argue. Now I realize you were trying to speak to me from the heart about what's most important to you, and I refused to listen.
>
> All of this tears me apart. We've become close these past few years, but I was so into Mary's appearances that I ignored the woman you've become. Now the two of you are in holy alliance.

I don't mean to sound self-pitying, but there's a lot I don't understand. During the appearances I became Mary and she became me. I internalized her sorrow over the state of Earth. Her sense of urgency became my sense of urgency. Once she took off, though, I was left with only myself. How is it that by myself I'm a coward?

Please, please. I want you to be a coward too. I'll say again how much I love you.

Mom

"HELP," SHE HEARS. "Get me out of here." Even if somebody broke the glass, she would never be able to escape. Her robe has to weigh at least a ton, and Jesus' body—how heavy is it?

"I've got a cramp in my right leg," she complains. So she's not eternally patient, Elizabeth thinks. Just eternal, created of marble by a man who earned immortality as well.

"It's all a trap, the perpetual youthfulness, the idealized beauty. Youth and beauty are not eternal. And who would want them to be? Who wants to sit perfectly still while others enjoy the pleasures of living? At least take him off my lap, will you, so I can sip espresso in the piazza. I want to sit on a rock by the sea and smell the salt and watch the gulls dive for fish. I want to..."

Elizabeth consults her travel guide. Michelangelo said of this work, "Chastity enjoys eternal youth." She wonders if that isn't what all boys want to believe about their mother: that she is, first of all, chaste. Secondly, that she is eternally young, which is supposed to be synonymous with beautiful. If there's a clue here explaining Randy's enduring fury, it escapes her.

Trapped in marble to satisfy the sculptor's own longings. Michelangelo even signed his name, which the guide book says he did in none of his other works. *You are mine*, his signature upon his mother's breast seems to claim.

"You must leave now," a guard says. "His Eminence is coming, and we must vacate the premises." Elizabeth looks around and sees that the basilica, which an hour earlier was swarming with guides explaining to their disciples in a variety of languages the magnitude and history of Saint Peter's, is now practically empty.

As she walks away she turns around for one last look. It occurs to her that the many folds in Mary's garment were needed to support Jesus' weight, making him appear small by comparison. The way a mother always remembers her child. As Elizabeth pictures Randy and Angelica. The darling little boy who loved to sit on her lap, who for more than a year insisted on wearing a string headband around his curly auburn hair. Carrying a bucket half his size he'd follow Wendell, pretending to be a farmer too. When he wasn't pretending to be a firefighter or doctor. And the precious little girl. So bright, so curious, so concerned about every injustice. "It's not fair," Angelica used to say. "Do something." How often the family frantically searched the barn, the chicken coop, only to find her sitting on the ground between rows of corn or up in the willow or wild cherry tree. Yes, even in adulthood they're Elizabeth's little boy and little girl.

SHE'S SQUEEZED ON A BENCH along the wall, between a rotund American man who can't whisper—but then, who in here is whispering?—and a Japanese woman with earphones. Both of them, necks craning, gaze up at the ceiling while she stares toward the front in disbelief.

It's as if Michelangelo painted her father on the altar wall from a photograph: the receding hairline and pouting mouth. Sorrowful eyes pleading for her to rescue him.

*Me rescue you? I didn't create your world, you had choices. You're the one who picked Armageddon as your hometown, your Bible always open to Revelation. Anti-Christ, end time, wailing and gnashing of teeth. All the time wanting Earth to be in chaos, burn up, destroy itself so that Jesus will come. And where did it get you? Where has it gotten Earth?*

It's a disturbing scene, though, Vernon suspended between heaven and hell, the expression on his face, like that of others at the bottom of the mural, of anguish. She doesn't want the sadness that haunted him on earth to last for eternity. *Please, angel—yes, you, right above him—reach a little further, grasp his arm, reach farther, farther. Pull him toward you, yes, that's the way.*

Vernon's face is bathed in calmness. He's smiling. Her father is actually smiling.

She leaves the Sistine Chapel without ever looking up at the ceiling, without even a glimpse of Father God creating Father Man.

MONDAY AFTERNOON. She planned the day all wrong. Rather, she didn't plan the day, and this is the result: everything's closed. Churches, museums, everything. She tells herself to just accept it, go sip a glass of wine in a cafe overlooking a fountain, and relax a little. Instead, she walks.

It's a residential neighborhood. Compared to the ancient churches she's been in, the buildings are recent. 1886 is on a plaque. She's thinking she'd like to live here, spend evenings in this small piazza with the trickling fountain. Maybe if she finds Mary in Rome, Mary will insist on staying. Elizabeth could learn Italian, get more comfortable with the transportation system. She could buy a simple building and turn it into a bed and breakfast. For women traveling alone. It wouldn't take much to make it more hospitable than the convent. Mary would stop by every now and then.

Elizabeth walks down a narrow street, thinking that if she stays she'll have to figure out how women hang their clothes on the lines stretching from one second-story window to the next. Turning the corner she finds herself at a dead end. In front of her, built into the wall of an apartment building, is a shallow alcove. Inside it there's a mosaic of Mary holding her child. On the ground two vases contain once-fresh red and pink gladiolus, now withered with brown edges.

The child has blond hair. Far too large for any woman not into body building to hold in the crook of her right arm. Mary's left hand clasps the edge of her robe, as if about to open it. He's just announced, I'm hungry, Mom. Give me some milk. Instead of looking disgusted and saying, if you're big enough to ask for it, you're big enough to drink it out of a cup, she's about to bare a breast. This being a dead-end street, there's no one except Elizabeth to see it right now.

Based on the little she remembers from high school Latin, she interprets the words below the mosaic to mean Mother of Divine Love. Somebody understands. Mary is not to be honored because she was pure enough to be chosen to be Jesus' mother but because she loved all of her children, the girls as much as the boys.

This is not Mary and Jesus but Mary and her daughter Hannah, and she's called Mother of Divine Love because she's wanting a better world for her daughters. She wants her daughters to be free of the colonizer who says your labor belongs to me, your body belongs to me, you are only fit for the church kitchen. You cannot question our doctrines. You cannot be part in our fellowship.

Elizabeth kneels before the shrine.

# A Vision

*For thou art with me. For thou art with me. Elizabeth. Elizabeth. Look for Joseph in Rome. Father Joseph Finotti. Look in the cafes. Look along the river, the crowded buses. Not in sacred sanctuaries but where people gather. The community gossips about us. The bishop moves him up North. I have sinned, I acknowledge in confession. Does he also state the truth to his confessor? John plans to build an inn and tavern, assuming I will carry the burdens of hospitality. Darkies will, of course, do much of the work, he assures me, but I am certain unsavory elements will frequent such an establishment. The drunkenness, the noise—how will this be suitable surroundings in which children grow up? I hear Joseph's comforting voice in his letters, his Italian accent stressing the wrong syllables. He trusts that my piety will influence the children to follow the ways of the Lord. Look for Joseph. For thou art with me. For thou...*

# Chapter 7

T HE FRONT WINDOWS of what had obviously once been a corner filling station now exhibited faded color photos of property for sale. I read the banner above the pictures: "Enjoy the fresh air of Glen Ayre."

Just inside the door a depression in the green indoor-outdoor carpeting exposed black rubber padding. Two large oak desks were situated on either side of the wide room. At the unoccupied one, paper weights held down stacks of paper fluttering in gusts of frigid air blasted by a droning window air conditioner. Upon my entry a young woman at the other desk, surely just out of high school, put down her emery board. She stopped chewing her gum and stared at me.

"I want to buy the farm up on Crabapple Road," I blurted.

I made a futile attempt to sweep back wisps of faded red hair that had escaped the loosened knot barely gripping the back of my head. Tried to brush away burrs and dirt still clinging to the sticky apple pie residue on my clothing. "I know, I look terrible."

Mouth agape, eyes behind thick glasses wide in disbelief, the receptionist said nothing.

"Like I slept in this. Actually I did. Slept in my truck." Not waiting for an invitation, I wedged my frame into the narrow chair beside the desk. "You know, you can't really be sure about a place until you've slept there, find out whether or not you're restless. Slept like a puppy next to its mama's teat, I did, wasn't afraid of anything. I felt—I guess you could say I felt protected. You know what I mean?"

"N-n-not really." A panicked cry: "Daddy!" Somewhere behind a wood paneled wall a toilet flushed. A tall middle-aged man with a bushy mustache materialized. Wearing a pin-striped vested suit, he walked with the pelvic tilt of an ostrich, his posterior following his torso at a distance. Seeming unselfconscious of his humorous bearing, he carried himself with an air of self-importance. "Uh, Daddy, uh, Mr. Gardner, this woman is interested in seeing the Groskirk place."

"No, I'm not interested in seeing it. I want to buy it."

The receptionist rose and walked away from her desk. Mr. Gardner took her seat.

"How do you do, uh, Missus uh…" He leaned forward and extended his hand then seemed to think better of it.

"Elizabeth. Call me Elizabeth. I want to buy the farm on Crabapple Road."

He spoke as if talking with a child: very slowly, very clearly. "But, uh, Elizabeth, you don't even know how much it costs, and you haven't been inside. How do you know you can afford it?"

"Let me worry about that. It looks like I ought to be able to move in right away."

Mr. Gardner seemed to be torn between making an easy sale and ethical behavior. But only briefly. Less than five minutes later he was filling out forms in triplicate. Convincing myself that I deserved a reward for more than twenty years of hard work, I wrote a check that completely wiped out Wendell's and my joint bank account.

Looking down at the hand that had just signed the check and papers, I suddenly felt empowered. I thrust out my bosom, wiggled my body out of the chair, and stood to my full height. I, no one else, not my father or Wendell, was determining the direction my life would take.

I SAT ON THE BACK STOOP, my skirt forming a trough between bent legs. Elbows digging into my thighs, chin resting in the cup of my hands, I listened while animals, accustomed to the absence of humans, freely communicated with each other. From tall grasses and from under buildings, their rustles, clinks, and caws announced, *This is my territory, this is my territory.* Down by the pond a croaking chorus of bull frogs signaled evening's arrival.

I looked out over my property. Its boundaries were wooded, young trees merging with the forest that ascended the knoll and continued up the mountain. Somewhere up there a spring gurgled from a crevice, waters wending their way down to create the narrow stream bed, blocked on my property by an earthen dam to form the pond. Between woods and land close to the house lay uncultivated fields, their former crops unknown. I'd have to do some research, determine the best use of the land.

To my right, a short distance from the house, a garden had once grown. Wendell's mother, in the brief time we had before she died, taught me how to garden then freeze and can its bounty. Come spring I'd expand the plot, hire somebody to break and till the soil. As I'd done up in Virginia, I would plant enough food to put away and last a year. The overgrown orchard—I could wait until late in the winter to prune tree branches. The barn, gray weathered sides leaning, would have to be torn down. The chicken coup could be salvaged, though its future use wasn't apparent. Maybe I'd get chickens, maybe I wouldn't. In any case I'd put a new roof on it and give it a couple of coats of white paint.

The main section of the house was a sturdy frame structure, but an addition on the back had transformed it into an architectural nightmare. Covered in pastel green aluminum siding, the appendage looked like a cheap motel, with four rooms all in a row connected by a windowless hallway. At the end of the hallway a door opened to the outside. The addition didn't have a source of heat, but since I had no ideas for its immediate use, I planned to shut the door between it and the main part of the house.

Doubt suddenly overcame me. I was by myself, with no one to share the burden of ownership. Fifty-seven years old, not too old for the strenuous work that would be required, but overweight, easily winded. I lowered my gaze to the cracked cement step my feet rested on. Instead of crying, as I felt like doing, I took a deep breath.

Raising my head I was startled to see a massive black bear lumber toward me. Step following step, it approached. Closer, closer, until its brown snout and the brown patches beside its black beady eyes became visible. My instinct told my to jump up and run into the house. Instead I remained sitting, meeting the bear's gaze. It stopped and raised itself on its hindquarters, displaying its sharp claws.

"I have no intention of taking over your home," I assured the bear. "I just want to start a new life here, that's all. We can share it, can't we?"

*Your home.* The words echoed in my mind. *Where you sleep, where you gather acorns and berries, where you give birth to your young. I'm an intruder, as of now without—so I have a house and property. How does a woman, by herself, make a home of all this?*

"But I promise I'll honor the land," I said aloud. Whether to myself or to the bear was unclear.

The bear dropped to all fours and, as if bowing, brought its snout down to the ground. Giving me a final stare, it turned and ambled past the garden area and chicken house, uphill, in the direction of the forest. I watched until its dark fur merged with evening shadows.

The setting sun painted the heavens to the west with brilliant streaks of pink and orange, turning the mountains into cobalt-hued silhouettes. Impulsively, I stood. Lifting my arms I began to sing a hymn I'd long ago learned at church: "God, who touchest earth with beauty, make me lovely too."

Twice I repeated the first stanza. "Recreate me," I sang. "Recreate me." Each time my voice became stronger, more fervent. When my body seemed no longer able to confine the polarities of joy and sadness, fear and confidence, I sank backward onto the ground. I gazed up into the day-releasing sky, arms resting beside me, palms open, my waist-length hair of faded orange-red unbraided, its crimped strands spread out.

I continued to lie there as the sun disappeared. The darkness of the valley and heavens merged; the crisp evening air added intensity to the brilliance of the stars. Gazing upward, I found myself among them, bounding from one to another, my body born by a sling of fabric.

A familiar scent came to me, a Christmas tree fragrance that took me back, back, back to the candle I had placed beside the Mary figurine when I was a girl. Back to the times, when from the corner of my bedroom ceiling Mary praised my intellect and said I reminded her of her daughters.

It took a moment for me to return to Earth, to sit up and catch my breath. I blinked in an effort to refocus my eyes on something that wasn't light years away, not knowing what to expect, yet...

"Hello, Elizabeth." Mary stood in a shaft of light, her streaked black and gray hair pulled back, hoop earrings hanging from her lobes. She wore a muslin peasant blouse and a full skirt that came to a few inches above her ankles. "I'm glad you're doing fine here."

I gasped for breath. "If you...if you can call...deserting my family...and, and...I blew it all up...everything." I lifted my arms and threw my hands wide. "Bghughgh! I've left all that's familiar for, for... I don't even know what for. The kids, they're going to hate me. And Wendell, he doesn't deserve this."

Forgetting that moments earlier I'd felt the exhilaration of bungee jumping through the Milky Way, I buried my face in my hands. "On top of it all, I've gone and—what a dumb-ass decision. What made me think I can simply buy this place and transform it into a—into a...None of this makes any sense."

A sweep of Mary's hand indicated the land beyond the small farm. "The forest over there. Lightning struck and fire consumed the trees. But the intense heat freed the seeds. They became the pines that now stand tall."

She held up the piece of fabric that moments earlier had supported me in the heavens. "See this?" It glowed in the light Mary radiated: strands of red and orange like the evening sun; rough, uneven threads of brown and rust, like the soil; and a large band of bold blue like the sky on a cloudless day. Gold threads ran through it. "It is Cloth of Terra. Spread it as a tablecloth, welcoming all who accompany Earth."

"But, but—why—why—after all these years, why are you here?"

She was gone.

I looked down to see the fabric wrapped under my arms, across my breasts. Rubbing its edge against my cheek I felt its roughness and strength.

During adolescence, plodding through big words and convoluted sentences of thick volumes checked out of the

Orlando Public Library, I had learned that people who hear voices are mentally ill. I chose an alternative explanation, that the voices I heard were a child's fantasy, Mary's visits an emotional crutch for a misfit at school, for a girl at odds with her father and punished for blasphemous questions at home.

I had pushed Mary away (though a few other voices intruded now and then). I transformed myself into the obedient daughter my father expected, later the woman the church expected, the wife Wendell expected. I shut myself off from what lies beyond the five senses.

What effort it took, trying to conceal my true nature. I became a woman out of sync with herself, unable to discern my rightful place. Submerging such a significant part of who I was, I became unknown even to myself.

Under the Milky Way's canopy, the recognition of all this swept over me. I vowed to abandon the former Elizabeth, the false self, but had not the vaguest notion of how to free the authentic one.

ON A SUNDAY MORNING, while Wendell and the kids attended church, I drove the Chevy pickup truck back up to Virginia. I planned to quickly gather a few clothes, books, and documents such as my birth certificate and Social Security card. I'd be back on the road by noon, before anyone got home. In case somebody drove by—though everyone I knew would be in church—I parked in back, near the door leading into the kitchen.

Out of habit my eyes scanned the kitchen counter, making sure it was tidy, everything put away. Instead, food residue stuck to the countertop, and the sink was filled with dirty dishes. A jarring reminder that Wendell needed me.

I felt only a little sentimental walking through the brick farmhouse where I'd lived more than twenty-five years. For the most part, furnishings were functional: a sofa and chairs for sitting, beds for sleeping, a table for eating. In many households decorative wall hangings or knick-knacks might have inspired a sense of nostalgia, but the Community of Brothers disapproved of ornamentation. Pretty objects were *of the world.*

Passing through the living room I noticed new magazines had arrived. Scattered on the coffee table were *Christian Home, Christian Woman,* and *Beef Farming Today.* Also a recent issue of *The Meisterfeld Alumni Update,* which Wendell always read from cover to cover. Having attended Meisterfeld only two years, I didn't usually pay much attention to the magazine. Once, though, I read in the obituaries that Tommy McCafferty had been killed in a car accident. I lost my virginity to him, underneath a church altar with "Do this in remembrance of me" engraved on the front.

I had no idea how Wendell organized papers and documents. He managed the family business: the breeding, feeding, and sale of livestock at the most profitable time; the planting and harvesting of crops. Like a piece of farm machinery, he required mainly fuel and maintenance. It had been my responsibility to place substantial meals on the table and keep his clothes clean and in good repair.

In his office, an alcove off the living room, I stood at the file cabinet, my hands fumbling through manila folders.

11:39. My Social Security card turned up in a file labeled "Tax Documentation." No sign of my birth certificate. I dumped dresser drawer contents, underwear mostly, into a paper bag, grabbed four pair of polyester pants. I rushed through the kitchen with my first load for the truck.

11:45. Church would be letting out soon. I rummaged through my sweater drawers. From a hanger in the hall closet, I seized my winter work jacket, my boots from the closet floor. I paused to consider my Sunday coat. No, I couldn't imagine myself going to church anymore.

11:47. Again I passed through the kitchen, arms barely able to reach around the bulky work jacket, boots, gloves, and heavy sweaters. On the counter I caught sight of my metal recipe box, with its rust-pocked pictures of double-crusted pies and tiered cakes. Since my adolescence it had been a treasured object, tied to the only skill I had: cooking. To leave that identity felt like the whack! of a cleaver against a slab of beef.

Using my chin to balance the load, I grasped the box with my right hand and placed it on top of the winter clothes. I passed the refrigerator. Magnets stamped with "God bless our home" and "This is the day that the Lord hath made" held the kids' school photos in place. I reached for the pictures. The magnets supporting them clattered to the floor.

I could blame the rush I was in, or the habit of picking up fallen objects. As I leaned over, the recipe box, precariously perched on top of the winter clothes, began a slow descent. I tried to stop it with my chin. Too late. It hit the vinyl floor with a thud. The top flew open, index cards scattered. Ones on which I had painstakingly written recipes for rhubarb cheesecake, Sister Minnie's peach-blueberry cobbler, chocolate chip cinnamon rolls, and vegetarian dishes for Angelica.

I couldn't help myself. I thrust my face into the armload of clothes and began to sob into the sleeve of my winter jacket. Why couldn't this be easier?

No, there wasn't time for tears. I hurried into the living room and dropped the clothes on the sofa. Back in the kitchen, I squatted to collect the recipe cards, stuffing them and the metal box in a canvas bag. With the bag dangling from my arm, I returned to the living room to gather my clothes.

I stopped abruptly. A family portrait, with its Olan Mills blue background, hung on the wall behind the sofa. During the three years since it had been taken, Randy had grown taller than Wendell, Angelica had moved beyond pre-teen. The picture didn't show the change in me, whatever had been eating away inside me like a tapeworm.

Pictures! I wanted more than the ones from the refrigerator door.

12:02. I left the pile of clothes, the recipe box, and the school pictures on the sofa. I climbed the stairs as fast as I could, panting when I reached the top. In the upstairs hall closet I kept a box of photos I'd long intended to organize in an album but had never gotten around to. I grabbed a handful of pictures.

12:10. Church would be letting out by now.

I didn't intend to kidnap the family pet. As I opened the truck door to climb in, Jezebel jumped in the cab and refused to budge, even when I took the time to place her favorite canned dog food in her bowl. I reminded myself that I had been the one to feed the dog, remove ticks, and arrange vet appointments. I drove off, the Irish Setter riding erect in the passenger seat, the bowl of dog food still on the stoop, untouched.

"Rock of ages, cleft for me," I began to sing so loudly that Jezebel's eyes shifted from the roadside to stare at me. "Let me hide myself in Thee; Let the waters and the blood/From thy wounded side—Oh, lordy, get the Brothers' songs out of my brain."

BACK ON MY NORTH CAROLINA FARM I sorted through the booty. I stuffed clothes in the chest of drawers, dropped my Social Security card into the shoe box containing papers related to buying the property. Seated on the sofa, I looked at pictures I'd hastily gathered. One was of my parents, brother, and me in front of our Orlando home. I studied it, searching for clues that might explain who I had become.

I would have been about twelve, my breasts little nubs under the bibbed bodice of the floral-print cotton dress, which like Mama's came to mid-calf. My hair was in pigtails, with stray wisps. Mama had thick eyebrows and peasant cheeks. Her dark hair was parted in the middle, tightly pulled from her face. Daddy, with his large stature, dominated the frame. Like the subjects of old-time photographs, he kept a somber expression. His wire-framed glasses rested crookedly on his narrow nose. The pockmarks on his cheeks were barely visible. Daniel, who must have been nine or ten, squinted into the camera. As if to prevent him from bolting, Daddy's massive hands rested on his shoulders.

Mama, more than a head shorter than Daddy and standing with her shoulder behind him, appeared almost insignificant. If I resented Daddy's control, how did she feel? Daniel? He seemed to have taken up Daddy's mantle. He'd become a minister and with his wife and two kids moved out to Oregon to establish a new church. Every now and then I received a flyer about an evangelistic meeting he held. Other than that our communications were limited to Christmas letters.

While Mama, Daddy, and Daniel appeared connected in the picture, I stood slightly to the side, touching no one. Some might look at the pose and assume it was out of choice. When what I really wanted, I now saw, was for someone in the family to pull me closer.

Only Mary, who spoke to me from the corner of my bedroom ceiling or from a branch of the backyard grapefruit tree, understood my need for connection.

I'D ALREADY TAKEN the unforgivable step of depleting Wendell's and my checking account. What about the trust fund Grandma Gilbert had set up? My maternal grandparents had done well by investing in Florida real estate in the scrublands of Central Florida. Foolish purchases, everyone who knew them assumed. Until Disney bought it all. Apparently wealth offered too many temptations to be *of* the world. They built a humongous house with a swimming pool, bought a Cadillac, and left the Community of Brothers to join the Episcopalian Church. This final action drew the condemnation of my mother, Aunt Clara, and their husbands.

At Grandma Gilbert's funeral the minister said, "In my father's house are many mansions," but my grandmother already had a mansion, and she was so mad at everybody in the family that she left it to a local art group and established trust funds for grandchildren that couldn't be accessed until we were thirty-five. Mom and Aunt Clara got nothing.

Wendell was adamant that we save my share for retirement. Yet, I now reasoned, he had the farm. And hadn't my efforts contributed to the farm's success? And wouldn't the land offer him a lifetime income? The only reason not to claim my inheritance… No good reasons came to mind. Still, I spent sleepless nights wrestling with my conscience before finally contacting the Orlando bank that served as trustee.

I bought an old tractor and mower at a public auction. In bib-overalls, t-shirt, and a straw hat, I bushwhacked the slope leading down to the pond. The task requiring the most immediate attention, though, was preparing the garden for the following spring. I hired Hank Lavernik, a farmer who lived down the road, to plow the large plot and spread manure. From the narrow copse of oak and hickory trees north of the house, I hauled load after load of leaves in a crude wagon pulled by the tractor. After shredding them and spreading them on top of the manure, I set about the back-straining job of working the manure and leaves into the clay soil with a pitchfork.

All the while bellowing hymns so loudly that Jezebel eyed me suspiciously. "Lead on, O king eternal/The day of march has come. Henceforth in fields of conquest/Thy tents shall be our home." No, that was the Brothers' song. I needed some new ones that were mine. But I couldn't think of any and soon found myself working more manure and shredded leaves into the soil to the words of "Rise Up, O Men of God."

I still hadn't decided whether to raise chickens, though there was a well constructed hen house. The previous owners seemed to have used it as a repository for things they didn't know what else to do with: an enamel bedpan, a bottle for a kerosene stove, rusted tools with no identifiable function, a rotted canvas tent. In a nesting box a snake had shed its skin, the parchment cells loosely coiled, lifeless. I felt a kinship with the snake. Leaving the past, creating a future free of the old skin.

Meanwhile, Hank tore down the barn and stacked the planks for firewood. A few we reserved to become shelves for the pantry I wanted built in the kitchen. With the barn no longer there, the ancient oak tree next to it stood alone, an eerie figure with weary arms. Burls on its gnarled base suggested it to be the dwelling place of ghouls.

Occasionally I came upon bear scat. At other times I spotted a bear on its hind legs reaching for wormy apples in the orchard or lumbering up the hillside toward the forest. Jezebel's first encounter with one did not go well. A slap of the paw was all it took for the dog to run back to the house. After that, she whimpered on the stoop outside the kitchen when our visitor came by.

Dear Elizabeth Mattison:

Because our Lord and Savior said, "There is no divorce," and the Apostle Paul wrote, "What God hath joined together, let no man put asunder," the

Community of Brothers has from our inception believed and taught that divorce goes against God's will.

For that reason the Elder Board, after prayerful consideration, has voted to disfellowship you. That is, from this day forward, you will no longer be addressed as Sister. You are no longer allowed to partake in Holy Communion or join us in Sunday worship. Your name will not be spoken among us.

In prayer for your eternal soul, that you will renounce your sinfulness and return to your husband and children, we remain

Emanuel Larson, Elder Board Chairman<br>
Arlo Hudson, Recording Secretary


On the same day a second envelope arrived. Inside it a piece of lined paper torn out of a spiral notebook.


I hate you. No woman who loves her family would leave them like you left us. You are a total embarrassment and I hope you rot in hell.
Randy


I CRUMBLED THE LETTER from the Brothers and tossed it in the trash. I figured we'd given up on each other—the Brothers and I—long before now. But I continued to hold Randy's note, smoothing the page's torn edge between thumb and index finger, as if by doing so I might smooth the rift in our relationship.

I'd invested nineteen years in caring for him. Not begrudgingly, but because I loved him. I paced the floor with him when he was a colicky baby. I was the first to hug his drenched body when he took that first faltering step out of the baptistery. I'd held him in my arms when Allison McMillan broke up with him. I'd hired a tutor when he struggled with physics. I had seen to his physical needs too, made sure he was fed and clothed. Would he ever quit making demands of me?

Wendell had more reason to be angry. Yet in his phone calls he continued to whine: "Why didn't you tell me you were unhappy? I'd have changed." To which I couldn't adequately respond, even to myself.

The Brothers' contradictory messages must have confused him. While committed to male entitlement, they also quoted Jesus: "And him that taketh away thy cloak forbid not to take away thy coat also." Wendell agreed to a modest settlement.

Where did Angelica fit in our family drama? I wasn't sure.

# A Vision

*Thy rod and thy staff they comfort me. Thy rod and thy staff… Through a crack in my pulled draperies I view ignorant crowds gathering up and down H street, hobbled by grief when they should be celebrating. They do not understand, but the South will. Any day word will come that his death has given our forces new hope and Lee will forfeit the surrender. Desperado of the worst kind, what this morning's paper said about Johnny, assuming that his friendship with Wilkes makes him a participant in the plan. An insistent knock at the door. Five men, two in the uniform of Yankee officers. Southern men would not enter so rudely. They are taught from childhood to treat women with respect. Are you Mrs. Surratt, the mother of John Surratt, Jr.? I am. Where is he? I do not know, sir. When did you last see your son? Where is he? Where is he? Where is he? Many mothers do not know the whereabouts of their children, I tell them. With glaring eyes they seize Anna and me, speaking not of where they intend to take us. Hail Mary, full of grace…now and at the hour of our death. I keep my composure, but my poor Anna is distraught. From her birth I sheltered her, protected her from a father who too often popped a cork and from ruffians such as these agents of the devil. Dear daughter, be strong, be strong. Our hands tightly clasped, hers delicate, mine large and rough from a lifetime of physical toil. May I have a few moments to pray before we leave? I need the piano for support as I kneel. Father in heaven, please keep Johnny safe from harm. Whatever words come from my mouth, let them not endanger his life. Let me not disclose anything that will incriminate the others. Be with General Lee, President Davis, and all the poor boys captured by the Yankees. They are hungry and tired. And be with our beloved Confederacy. Though she has been defeated in battle, may she not be defeated in spirit. With Wilkes also. Keep him safe. Keep him safe. Our Father, who art in heaven, hallowed be thy name…Amen. Listen, Elizabeth. We cannot leave justice up to others. Thy rod and thy staff they…*

# Chapter 8

**ROME**

TWO AMERICANS HAVE BEEN KILLED on Borneo, the CNN anchorwoman announces from a TV screen on the opposite side of the bar. Perched on a padded stool in the long dark room, Elizabeth peers into the faces of a young couple. A wedding picture it seems, an event not marked by extravagance, as the groom wears an open-necked shirt, the bride a simple white sundress.

"Would you turn up the volume, please?" she asks the bartender.

That a hotel bar would be open this early in the morning is beyond her understanding. But the suspicious glare of the woman at the front desk gave her reason to saunter past the lounge she's claimed as her own since getting kicked out of the other hotel. To justify her presence here she sips from a glass of ginger ale. At the other end of the bar a middle-aged man with a mop of black and gray hair leans into a drink likely to offer more of a kick than ginger ale.

The camera pans acre upon acre of oil palm trees planted in uniform rows, then sweeps into the rainforest beyond. Comes to rest on a small settlement. Children outside a long, narrow building on stilts stare curiously into the lens An elderly man sits on a stool, boring the hole for what is identified as a blow gun.

"For generations the Dayak people have used this land for subsistence agriculture, hunting, and fishing," the reporter says.

But meeting the world's desire for palm oil is a lucrative business, Elizabeth learns. The owners of giant plantations continually encroach on the rainforest where the Dayak have lived for centuries, where they drained swamps for farmland, where they hunt.

The young American couple traveled to Malaysia in support of the indigenous people. In defiance of bulldozers the couple sat alongside the Dayaks in farmed fields, by the stream where the Dayaks fish, and in the surrounding jungle where they hunt. On the previous Sunday, though, while many attended church, the bulldozers approached. Thugs hired by plantation owners swung machetes.

The American couple and three Dayak men were killed.

The bartender, who's been wiping the same area of the counter ever since Elizabeth walked in, has turned his face toward the TV. He mumbles in Italian. It sounds like cursing. "No difference," he says in English, "they die. Big company always win."

The camera enters the settlement's main building, a longhouse it's called. Many apartments are connected by a wide enclosed porch running all the way across the front. While the tribe practices the old way of living together, the longhouse has indoor plumbing and electricity. All the people want, the reporter says, is to live their traditional life. Yet the global economy is making its way into these hinterlands, grabbing the Dayaks' rights over this land.

Elizabeth drinks the last of her ginger ale. The young American woman is someone's daughter, she thinks, her husband someone's son. Their lives taken because they joined the people in standing up to powerful plantation owners. The three Dayak men, each of them someone's son, someone's husband, someone's father. They died so their children might inherit the land of their ancestors.

Mothers of the young couple probably begged them not to go. There are cobras, they would have said, and mosquitoes that carry malaria. Somewhere out there Angelica, not unlike the young American woman and man, is standing up to corporations.


SHE'S UNPREPARED for the emotional impact. The giant fresco, Jesus's body being taken from the cross. Mary has fainted. Oh, Mother of Love, Elizabeth cries in her heart, how you suffered. To gaze upon the body of your executed son. To have witnessed his torture and abuse. His head hangs, his skin is ashen. Spear wounds mark his flesh. There's no trace of his once twinkling, intelligent eyes, no playful smile that only a mother is privy to. This is the boy you gave birth to, the son you nursed, who played by your side. In the past few days you have cried until no tears remain.

Your own son as much as he is God's. You, not God, taught him to speak and sing and dance. To take a woman's child, to fill that child with passion for a cause so much bigger than himself. To sacrifice him to the cause. If only I could have died instead, you wailed just before you fainted.

Elizabeth inhales the suffering as if it were the essence of existence. She falls to the kneeling bench, hands folded in prayer. *How much do mothers have to bear? Spare our sons and daughters.*

From the shadows a woman approaches, squats, and without speaking places a hand on Elizabeth's shoulder. Keeps it there until she's calmed. When Elizabeth stands to leave, the woman is gone.

To: wl83@torbox3.onion    Sept 25 7:31 AM
Subject: hi
Dear One,

Right now I'm remembering this date seven years ago. When I heard gravel crunching in the driveway, I assumed it was a customer. Instead, like circus clowns, you and your friends poured out of two cars, one kid even carrying a tuba. Jezebel howled while you all played Happy Birthday. It's a good thing I live in the country.

Though a day early, the marking of my advancing years didn't go unrecognized here either. Last evening I ate where I've gone three times before, at an outdoor restaurant near the Vatican. Each time the same young man's been my waiter. He must be a lonely person. He's rather unattractive, with a lopsided face and a paunch that hangs over his red cummerbund. A flower vendor walked from table to table, pressuring men to buy a rose for the woman they were with. My waiter bought one for me. I consider it a birthday gift.

Nowadays birthdays leave me wondering how many years remain. Ten? Twenty? Maybe tomorrow I'll get hit crossing a street. (Not unimaginable. Traffic here only stops for pregnant women.) I want to make a difference in the time I have left. While I worry about you and keep trying to change your mind (futilely, I know), I can't help but envy your commitment. Can a woman my age also dream of making a difference? Can a woman in her sixties find purpose? Mary gave me that purpose, but without her I flounder in my commitment.

I must remind myself, as I remind you, not all deeds of fervor achieve their goals. And, as I've said multiple times, I'm averse to risk. In any case I hope to celebrate the next birthday with you. No need for a band. Just you.

Love,
Mom

THE MAP DOESN'T SHOW elevations, so she doesn't anticipate that the trip to the Tempietto is all uphill. Or that she'll have to huff and puff her way up an interminable flight of steps ending at the edge of a heavily traveled roadway. Unable to see beyond bends in both directions, she listens for oncoming traffic, which, given this is Rome, isn't all that hard to hear. In a moment of relative quiet she darts across.

Getting up here has turned out to be an arduous trek for nothing. Like many structures and monuments, the Tempietto is closed for restoration. There's a neighboring building, though, a chapel, its open door inviting the weary to pause and rest.

She steps into a narrow anteroom. From the other side of the wooden petition comes a commanding male voice. She pokes her head through the doorway leading into the nave. The small church is filled with people, everyone standing with head bowed. In the front, past the ends of pews decorated with clusters of white flowers, a bride and groom kneel before a priest. The priest pauses; the congregation joins him in reciting what she's guessing is The Lord's Prayer. During the prayer a man with a video camera pans the wedding guests, lingering at the back of the chapel on Elizabeth, a woman neither the bride nor groom will recognize, a stranger wearing a hat with a wide brim, peeking around the door.

She's about to turn and go back outside when the sanctuary becomes silent. Any step on the aged wooden floor is certain to produce a loud creak. Her body tenses, waiting for a suitable moment to leave. Then, like a wood thrush's clear sweet song breaks into a still summer morning, a soprano voice fills the sanctuary with the melodious strains of "Ave Maria." The sacredness of the moment overwhelms Elizabeth. It is Mary's birthday gift to her, she's certain.

She wipes her tears with the sleeve of her blouse and turns to leave.

BY THE END OF THE FIFTH DAY, on the map given Elizabeth at the airport information kiosk, she's placed a checkmark beside each church she's entered. Meanwhile she's visited none of the usual attractions. A mistake, she decides.

Tourists point cameras at arches connecting nothing, at columns supporting nothing. Fragments of walls, ruin stacked atop ruin, ascend a hill. It's as if Elizabeth strolls the paths of an abandoned cemetery. Which it is: a monument to past lives.

She meanders along a grassy rectangle, studying the row of headless Vestal Virgins. Until she went to college, she expected to someday be rewarded for virginity. Had she maintained it—what woman can help but consider the might-have-beens?

A man stands beside the pedestal of the only virgin with a head. His feet are planted apart, his neck lifted upward in careful study of the figure. Elizabeth takes another look, notices his large frame, pocked cheeks, and the gray fringe of hair encircling a receding hairline. He wears khaki shorts and a yellow t-shirt, the word *Roma* above the Coliseum's silhouette.

"Daddy?"

"The most sacred of all the shrines," Vernon says, stepping toward her. His tone is instructive. "Six virgins served as priestesses and were responsible for keeping the eternal flame going. If they kept the vow of chastity thirty years, they lived a life of luxury. Break the vow, though, and they were buried alive, their lover flogged to death. The virgins were also punished if they let the light go out."

Elizabeth replies: "Seems not to have occurred to the priests that they could keep it going themselves. They thought there are certain jobs only a woman can do. I'll bet they kept blaming the virgins long after the flame went out permanently." She lowers the register of her voice to sound masculine. "Back in the old days we'd say we needed six virgins to keep the flame going and got six good candidates."

"Hmm," he says, "it reminds me of Jesus' parable about the wise and foolish virgins. I guess the new religion had to keep some of the trimmings of paganism so people wouldn't be upset. You bring over a few of the old ideas. You add a virgin to the mix."

"My, travel really does broaden the mind."

"One gains perspective on the Other Side."

"How so?"

"Well, I'd say I considered important what should not have been. As if God appointed me to keep track of everyone's sins."

This is her father? Vernon Pierson? Husband of Barbara Pierson? Father of Daniel Pierson and Elizabeth Pierson Mattison McNair? The man who dominated her childhood with his strict theology, large stature, and booming voice? Who bent her to his will until she had no sense of who she was?

"The thought occurs to me," he says, his hazel eyes playful, "I might have saved you a lot of heartache if I'd presented you as a Vestal Virgin at a young age. Put somebody else in charge of your upbringing. You know, as priestesses the women were allowed a lot of independence."

"I would have appreciated some independence. But eventually I probably would have defied authority and ended up wandering the field of the wicked with just a candle and a loaf of bread."

She and her father laugh in unison. Yes, he laughs.

# Chapter 9

HAD HE WORN A FUR-TRIMMED RED CAP to conceal his baldness, Hank Lavernik would have resembled Santa Claus: round of belly, with a white beard. Though a resourceful man, Hank occasionally gave the bottle priority over work he'd agreed to do, extending what might have been a two-or-three-day project into one requiring a week or more. I worried how his wife, Ethel, coped at these times.

When winter brought fewer than eight hours of daylight to the southern Appalachians and temperatures dropped, Hank and I transferred our efforts indoors. Working together, seldom speaking, we opened the space between living room and kitchen, tearing out cabinets, putting in a peninsula. Under moldy carpeting we discovered wide-planked oak floors. Painting came next, beginning with the upstairs bedrooms, mine and a guest room intended for Randy's and Angelica's stays. So far their visits seemed unlikely.

I can't say where the idea came from, the need for a sacred space. In my bedroom, next to a long, narrow window facing the mountains to the east, I draped Cloth of Terra, folded multiple times, over a round wicker table. On top of the fabric, I placed a candle and a blue geode. I had no idea how to pray, or to whom. Not to the God of the Brothers, for sure. In my rocking chair, body leaning forward then back, forward again, I came to experience the chair's rhythms as a conduit to an inner harmony I'd not known before.

Yet sometimes, especially when my thoughts turned to Randy's note, I lapsed into self-blame. Why couldn't I have been a better mother? Why couldn't I honor my marriage vows? Wendell wasn't an abusive husband. My biggest complaint was that he snored at night, but no woman would leave her husband simply because he snored. Why couldn't I be satisfied just to be a farmer's wife and the mother of Randy and Angelica?

When the kids were little, the pressure cooker I inherited from Wendell's mother blew a gasket, sending apple sauce shooting up like a geyser. Now I felt like apple sauce up on the ceiling. Stuck there until somebody scrubbed it off. No, I was the pressure cooker, and the mess on the ceiling was my fault.

At the end of each day, feet propped on the worn leather ottoman—purchased along with the rest of my furniture at a public auction—I would fall asleep in front of the wood-burning stove. Around midnight I roused myself, scattered the coals, and turned off the floor lamp next to the sofa. With Jezebel padding behind me, I climbed the stairs. Lying in bed I listened to owls beyond the frosted window, calling back and forth, defining their territory.

I awakened when dim traces of daylight hovered over the valley. A fire in the stove, a cup of coffee, a bowl of oatmeal, and I was ready to take Jezebel for a walk. Before us and behind, the mountains were shrouded in morning mist. Sometimes rime ice clinging to tree branches sparkled in the early sun. On the coldest days ice formed on the pond's surface.

I wondered about the animals who, upon my arrival, had been freely clicking and clacking. A few lingered, especially feathered ones. Doves and juncos ate the cracked corn I scattered on the ground, and red-tailed hawks perched on the highest branches of bare trees, their piercing eyes searching for prey. Once in a while Jezebel and I followed paw tracks through snowdrifts. Most likely the unfeathered wintered in the cracks of boulders, under rocks, in the ground. And my bear visitor? Was it asleep up on the mountain? Would it return in the spring?

Other than red berries clustered around the bright green leaves of holly trees and occasional animal tracks in the snow, life seemed suspended. In retrospect I understand that the dormancy of winter is necessary for the blossoms of spring and the fruits of summer.

It usually didn't bother me that much of my time was spent alone. My previous life had been too full of interaction: teaching children's Sunday school classes, going to monthly meetings of

Ladies' Aid, attending church services twice on Sunday and during the week. Every day farm hands had sat at our kitchen table, eating food I'd prepared. It had been my responsibility to make sure Randy and Angelica did their chores and homework and were transported to wherever they needed to go.

Sometimes Hank, even when there wasn't a project, stopped by. Strange visits, they were, since neither of us had much to talk about, just sat in the living room listening to logs sizzle in the wood stove. Agnes, the mail carrier, if I was pruning apple trees or working near the road, would lean out the white truck, ask *How ya doin?* then proceed to tell me that the Carters, down the valley, had a new baby girl, or that the Monroe boy stepped on a nail, went clean through his boot.

And there were bi-weekly trips to Asheville or Johnson City for supplies, depending on my preference at the time. Store clerks often initiated a conversation about the weather or pointed out that while the generic brand of oatmeal was all right, Quaker was on sale that week. They'd hold up a line of customers while I made my way to the cereal aisle and back.

Some days, though, I felt an intense loneliness. I missed my family. When I called back to Virginia, a lump of near-remorse lodged in my throat. In my head my own voice bounced against the walls of my cranium, sounding distant, like it belonged to someone else. After a while Wendell's tone became businesslike. Angelica was so overcome by sniffles that phone conversations contained extended silences. Randy, if he was home from Virginia Tech, refused to talk.

And I missed having someone to cook for. My Virginia kitchen had been a welcoming place, with wreaths of herbs and the fragrances of baking bread or cakes or pies. The farm hands had been an appreciative audience for creamy gravies and rich desserts. Now new eating habits lessened my own pleasure at mealtime. No desserts, red meats, or processed foods. Mainly green and yellow vegetables, beans, cheese, and whole grains. My puffy cheeks and prominent jowls began to shrink, my polyester pants with an elastic band hung on me.

One day late in January Hank returned from a trip to Knoxville with a shotgun. A Remington 870. Pump action and a short-enough barrel. For protection against intruders, he said, a woman living alone. And to scare off bears and coyotes and wild boars coming down from the forest.

I wasn't a stranger to guns. Wendell had one. Several times he shot foxes prowling around the chicken coop. He gave the tails to Randy, who attached them to the back of a baseball cap. Angelica offered the tailless predators proper burials out beyond the garden, lifting prayers on behalf of the foxes' souls and singing between sniffles, "In the sweet by and by we shall meet on that beautiful shore."

Down in North Carolina, I felt no danger. I could never bring myself to harm a bear. A boar maybe, not a bear. I wondered whether, given the right circumstances—though I couldn't imagine what they might be—could I take a human life?

READY FOR BED—IN flannel pajamas, a robe, and insulated slippers—I returned the toothbrush to its holder. I paused to study my reflection in the mirror. Brought my fingers to the large sun spot on my right cheek, my faded rust-colored eyebrows that had never been plucked. I pulled the braid hanging down the center of my back to the front. *It's as if your head were shaved,* Brother Baker had exhorted from the pulpit. *It's as if your head were shaved. If you don't wear the covering, it's as if your head were shaved.* With both hands I moved my fingers up and down the braid's ridges. In TV ads men gazed admiringly at women whose silky long hair floated in the breeze. Women, don't draw attention to your hair—that's what the church taught. It's your fault if a Brother lusts after you. Not that I believed for a minute that anyone lusted after me.

My slippers made a flopping sound as I descended the stairs. In the chill of my living room, the only light coming from a small lamp on the end table, I reached into my sewing box. The scissors were on the bottom. I clicked them open and together. Open and together.

I took a seat on the worn leather hassock in front of the sofa, still clicking the scissors. By now Jezebel stood in front of me, gazing up into my eyes, trying to understand what was going on.

As was I—trying to understand. One truth seemed clear: my uncut hair bound me to the Community of Brothers.

How many times as a girl had I sat on the vanity bench in my parents' bedroom while my mother brushed the tangles out, as I, a mother myself, later brushed Angelica's hair? A mother's job, it is, freeing her daughter of tangles. That was at the heart of my present dilemma, wasn't it? Could I free myself of tangles? Was it possible to free myself from Sisters and Brothers so central to my identity?

The sharp crotch of the scissors pressed against my braid. A single vigorous snip was impossible. I sawed away, severing a few strands at a time. Finally I grasped the shorn braid in the palm of my hand.

The next afternoon in Doris's Day Salon in Burnsville I pointed to a picture in one of her many style magazines. "Honey, are you sure you want a crew-cut?" Doris asked. Yes, positive.

The image in the mirror showed a middle-aged woman with a pleasantly round face and rosy cheeks. And very short hair, gray mixed with faded orange-red.

AREA LANDMARKS BECAME FAMILIAR. Down the road a junk yard stretched up the side of a hill, its stacked cars, school buses, and other refuse camouflaged in winter by rust-colored leaves persistently clinging to oak trees. Beyond the junk yard, a Full Gospel Church and adjoining cemetery. Farther yet, a cluster of mobile homes, one flying a tattered Confederate flag.

After the mobile homes a faded Pure Oil sign stood in front of an abandoned square building of river rock. Going by the sign always reminded me of a family trip from Florida to Washington D.C. in our '52 Chevrolet. We'd stop at filling stations like this one, where Daddy would say "Fill her up" to the attendant wearing a blue jumpsuit with grease stains. The attendant would check the oil and clean the windshields.

Continuing south along the valley floor, I regularly passed frame bungalows and well-kept homes of red brick. I peered down lanes leading to houses set in the middle of corn fields. Once in a while I'd drive winding roads up nearby mountain slopes to developments of vista-blessed homes built by affluent people from Florida and states up North.

One morning in early February, I'd driven past the junk yard, mobile home park, and Full Gospel Church en route to a grocery in Asheville that carried a wide variety of organic products. Back home I stacked cans of organic fruits and vegetables on pantry shelves, refrigerated perishables and stone-ground whole wheat flour. As Wendell's wife I'd put away enough garden vegetables to last through the winter. I had every intention of doing the same here. Seeds already sprouted in the cold frame.

My mother-in-law taught me to can, but what did other people do? Those who wanted to eat healthy? Young women with jobs came home from work to fix dinner and do laundry, keep up with their kids' activities. If they wanted healthy food for their families they didn't have time to go to Asheville or Johnson City, much less can or freeze vegetables.

The tacked-on wing in back of the house. What if I tore out the inside walls and made it one open space? What if…a natural foods store?

Bad idea. Even a fool knows the success of a retail business depends on location, location, location. Besides, I liked my new life: morning walks with Jezebel, daytime hours engaged in the physical tasks of renovating the house, evenings that started with reading then morphed into dozing by the stove.

Maybe, though, it was time to branch out, do something for people who lived beyond my little parcel of land.

While I'd been in Asheville the fire in the wood stove had died down. A chill permeated the house. I placed a log inside, stirred the coals before closing the door, took a seat in the recliner. Jezebel, who had been following me around, tags clinking, settled on her haunches next to the chair.

"There are people all up and down these hollows," I said directly to the dog. "A lot of outsiders vacationing, some moving here to retire. Hank's forever talking about too many new folks moving in. Like he's forgotten I'm one of them. Complains they want all the conveniences of city living."

I took the multicolored afghan from the back of the chair and wrapped it around my shoulders. A succession of pops from the stove startled me.

"A bad idea. Do-good intentions won't cut it. No way can I grow enough vegetables to sell. Manage a store on top of that? I've got better things to do with my time than sell groceries."

I ran my hand through Jezebel's chestnut fur. "Like what? What better things? I've been interested in food since high school. The preparation and the eating. I could sell my own baked goods. Who wouldn't rather have a homemade cake than a packaged one loaded with preservatives?

"No, it *is* a bad idea. What do I know about running a business? Wendell was the competent one. . . . On the other hand, I'm not stupid. I could learn. I could talk with some people." I slapped both thighs and stood. "Makes more sense than talking to a dog."

# A Vision

*I will fear no evil, for thou art with me. I will fear no… Even on Sunday men in uniform lead me from my cell, holding firmly to my arms as we make our way down a bare hallway to an office where a Yankee soldier interrogates me. His rank I do not know, but surely he is eminent. Again I am asked, Where is your son John? I gaze steadily into his eyes and assert that I do not know. Yes, I am acquainted with Mr. Booth. He came to the house, often when Johnny was not there. My calmness and poise impress even myself, though inwardly my stomach stirs and in my breast I feel the rapid pounding of my heart. Listen, Elizabeth. Women must become practiced in the art of concealment. I will fear no evil, for thou…*

# Chapter 10

IN ASHEVILLE I INTERVIEWED the owner of a store similar to the kind I envisioned. At Malaprop's I bought books about how to succeed as an entrepreneur. I spent hours at the round kitchen table with a pad of paper, pencil in my right hand, a calculator in front of me. The costs of commercial gardening: seeds, potting soil, soil nutrients—like bone meal, manure, lime—organic pest control, harvesting tools. Renovation expenses: insulation, wiring, shelving. I chewed on the pencil eraser as I studied the amount needed for an initial inventory. Opening a store would make a huge dent in the funds inherited from my grandmother, but the math showed it could be done, assuming I started out small.

In early March—with the first average frost-free date still almost two months away—I daily donned my fleece-lined corduroy jacket and wool cap. I steered the loaded wheelbarrow to the garden. Under the tutelage of my mother-in-law, I'd discovered my gift for growing vegetables. Here in North Carolina I had already tackled the hardest, most important task: the start of transforming clay into a nurturing womb. The time had come to plant potatoes and onions, transplant greens from the cold frame, get seeds for cold-hardy vegetables in the ground. Some seeds I scattered; others I placed in shallow furrows. Hunched over, I made my way up and down the rows. Jezebel mostly hung around, but the occasional sighting of a rabbit or chipmunk sent her racing across the garden, her grating bark interrupting the chickadees' *hey, sweetie.*

While I worked outside Hank began to tear down non-loadbearing walls inside the addition. He installed insulation, lighting, and a heat pump for heating and cooling the large open space. All I needed to say was, "I sure wish…" and he'd find somebody with the skills or inventory to satisfy me. I envisioned a massive weathered front door opening onto the gravel parking area. Hank bought one from an acquaintance who sold materials salvaged from razed buildings.

Week by week the bright green of new foliage gradually made its way up the hills, creeping layer above layer into the forest beyond. By late May mountain laurel was in full bloom, its white and pink clusters like cheerleaders' pompoms.

The bear had returned, twin cubs frolicking beside her. In a way mysterious to humans, she seemed at times to signal that they were to settle down and fall in line; this was a serious expedition in which they were to learn how to forage. Twice I saw angry yellow jackets attack. Mama Bear swatted at them with her paw while she dug for insect larvae with her nose.

While Hank worked on the addition—that is, on his sober days—I devoted most of my time to gardening. I built slatted pyramids for pea vines to climb, transplanted broccoli and cabbage from the cold frame, which still protected peppers, tomatoes, and eggplants. Kale and spinach were ready to be picked and eaten.

By June construction was near completion. Hank surprised me with an outdoor sculpture he'd welded from pieces of rusted metal: a woman with a large hat and bird feeders for hands. As non-perishable items began to arrive, I purchased advertising space in area newspapers, erected signs—one in front of the farm, seven others along the route—and delivered fliers all the way to Burnsville. To filling stations, restaurants, any place the public frequented.

*WILLOW POND NATURAL FOODS Store, Grand Opening,* the sign out front announced.

July first. I spent the day walking up and down the three long aisles, moving boxed cereals to a shelf more at eye level, relocating the canola oil to where the peanut butter had been, rearranging fresh organic vegetables. Not certain what the demand would be and with my garden not yet producing enough to sell, I'd purchased a small supply of vegetables from an established organic farm near Johnson City. Every now and then

I peered outside to see if I'd missed the sound of gravel crunching beneath car wheels.

July second. No customers. I spent most of the day perched on the stool behind the cash register, staring into space. I'd invested effort and money into a hopeless enterprise. What made me think I had the skills to start a business? What kind of incompetent woman would dare assume that valley residents and people beyond the valley would want a store like this? I should have known that any project of mine would be a disaster.

July third. No sense hanging around the store when the garden needed my attention. With crushed spirit I spread mulch among tomato plants, picked kale, and weeded between the green beans.

Not until July sixth did someone drive up the driveway. I dropped the hoe between rows of thigh-high corn, wiped my hands on my bib overalls, and ran from the garden to the store. I grabbed a clean white apron. I had my hands in the sink, scrubbing them with a stiff fingernail brush, when two women about my age entered.

They introduced themselves as Marguerite and Amelia. Of the two, Marguerite was the more gregarious, a tall, slender woman wearing cut-off jeans and a faded t-shirt. Amelia, standing slightly behind Marguerite, said little. Cake makeup covered a scar across her cheek, and she walked with a limp.

Between the freezer and check-out counter, I had created a hospitality corner: a small round table and four nail kegs topped with red cushions. Cloth of Terra covered the table. A pink impatiens plant in a small basket added a welcoming touch. Shyly I invited my first customers to sit and drink a glass of iced mint tea. Both left with a canvas bag full of groceries.

They returned the following day with three more women: Fran, Peaches, and Nada Sue. I rushed to the kitchen for two more chairs and extra glasses for tea.

Fran reminded me of the wind-up mouse Randy played with as a child, skittering across the room until it ran into the sofa, backing up an inch before taking off in another direction. Fran's heels tapped the floor, her fingers drummed on Cloth of Terra. Words escaped her mouth in staccato spurts. She lost no time in pressuring me to get involved in the local Democratic Party. I was too embarrassed to admit I'd always relied on Wendell to tell me who to vote for.

Peaches had a mountain drawl, sprinkled her talk with *Honey* and *Sugar* and *Bless her heart.* Yet she tossed out words I'd never heard before, like *paradigm* and *nihilism.* In college she majored in philosophy, I later learned.

Back in her high school days, Nada Sue must have ranked among the most popular girls. Even with graying hair, she still had a prom queen look—like a confection on lacy paper—and the kind of shapely body seen in magazine ads. She wore multiple rings and painted her fingernails bright red, making me self-conscious about my pudgy fingers and jagged fingernails. Though I was now free to adorn neck, wrists, fingers, and earlobes anyway I wanted, the only jewelry I owned was my wedding ring, tucked away in my underwear drawer.

Nada Sue was widowed, Marguerite and Peaches both married. Amelia was divorced. Fran made no bones about being a lesbian, which took me by surprise—her being unashamed, I mean, given my exposure to the Brothers' condemnation. None of the group seemed in a hurry to shop for groceries, just sat around the little table talking. Everyone but Amelia joked, cursed a little, got loud and argumentative. Unafraid of God's disapproval, it appeared.

I had just refilled iced tea glasses when Peaches lifted hers and said, "There is nothing with which every man—here I must substitute woman—there is nothing with which every woman is so afraid as getting to know how enormously much she is capable of doing and becoming. Soren Kierkegaard said that."

I was too embarrassed to ask who Soren Kierkegaard was.

"May your new business help you discover all you are capable of," Peaches continued.

The others lifted their glasses. "Hear, hear!"

Flustered by the attention, I lowered my eyes and said a muted "Thank you."

For more than an hour the five women sipped iced mint tea. When they finally got around to exploring the store, I heard

Marguerite point out free-range eggs, organic peanut butter, organic safflower oil. I heard the others' ahs of approval.

"We need to have a store blessing," Nada Sue said at the cash register. "You know, banish all evil, make your business prosper. How about Sunday? The store will be closed then, won't it?"

I nodded my head in the affirmative, though banishing evil wasn't part of my marketing plan.

THE SITUATION CONFUSED ME. With my little corner table and iced mint tea, I'd intended to offer hospitality. But the women had turned it all around. They became the hospitable ones, welcoming me into their circle. Should I think of them as customers, guests—was it too much to hope they'd be my friends? They were different from any women I'd ever known. Unlike the Sisters (and me, until now), they didn't seem cautious about what they said or how they appeared. They were…they were who they were.

To be their friend would surely require my authenticity as well. Authenticity? Everything about me had *former* attached to it: *former* wife, *former* farmer's wife, *former* member in the Community of Brothers, *former* Floridian, *former* Virginian. I wouldn't say *former* mother. A woman couldn't relinquish motherhood.

Already I knew I wanted to be one of these women *of* the world. I hoped they'd find me—the new me who wasn't yet sure what that involved—acceptable.

A DIFFERENT NADA SUE entered the store on Sunday afternoon. Not a confectionary homecoming queen but a woman whose stature seemed to have grown in the intervening days. Wearing a floor length cape of midnight blue over a matching long skirt, she walked with an air of authority.

She placed a bulky cardboard box next to the hospitality table. Withdrew a white pillar candle and a pale-blue pottery bowl. She handed the bowl to Marguerite. "Put water in this, would you, Sugar?

"Open all the windows," she told the rest of us. I considered objecting. Opening windows would let in humid air and contribute to mildew, but the others were already releasing latches, grunting as they lifted windows.

"Now, all y'all take one." She held out pie tins and metal spoons. I stood statue-like, staring at her, wondering if I should bring this nonsense to a halt.

She must have noticed my indecision. She clasped my hand. "Sugar, we're going to scare the evil spirits so much they're gonna fly out the window and not even think about coming back. Ever." She forcefully struck a pie tin with a metal spoon, an invitation for the rest of us to hit ours with equal fervor. Without any more hesitancy I stepped in line with the others. I hit the pie pan with the gusto of a one-year-old exerting her power. Soon we all marched behind Nada Sue, up and down store aisles, creating such a clanging racket that I wanted to put my fingers to my ears.

"Enough," she finally called out over the din. She extended both ringed hands, a signal to form a circle around the hospitality table, which held the unlit candle and blue pottery bowl.

"We are grateful that Elizabeth has chosen to live and work among us," she said. She smiled directly at me as she dipped her fingers in the water and scattered its spray into the air. She lit the candle. "Let this store remain a place of kindness, friendship, and hospitality."

"And turn a profit," Fran added. She reached across the table to press a wad of white tissue paper into my hand. "This is from all of us. Go on, see what's inside."

Self-conscious over being the center of attention, I pealed back layers of tissue. A miniature ceramic black bear nestled inside. "After the quiet of hibernation comes insight," I read aloud from a strip of paper. "Bear connects you to Earth and the heavens."

The Brothers would have disapproved of the store blessing. But some change in me took place during the clatter of pie tins and the lighting of the candle. A calming confidence in the future.

~~~
~~~

CLAIMING THE STORE FLOURISHED that first year would be an overstatement. But it generated enough income to pay the bills. I lived simply, with few needs. I wore faded bib overalls with flannel shirts in winter, with t-shirts in summer. Meals were simple fare, prepared from garden vegetables and dried beans.

Every now and then a note or card from Angelica arrived in the mail.

Dear Mom,

Thanks for the really great time. I'm sorry Randy was such a jerk. I guess it's going to be awhile before he forgives you, even though you apologized.

I'm glad your store is working out. I enjoyed learning to use the cash register and meeting interesting people. I like the farm a lot too, especially your pond, where I got to see so many interesting plants and animals. I used to want to be a vet, but after being there for a week, I'm thinking about becoming a biologist. I do well in my science classes at school.

I'll keep you informed.
Love,
Angelica

(a postcard)
Dear Mom, Greetings from camp. S. Eberhardt knows lots about wildlife & says I'm eager beaver. Saw eastern hellbender yesterday—crawls along river bottom. Keeping list of every animal I see.

Love you, A.

Dear Mom,

Thank you for the flower identification book. I've already taken it to the woods and identified a heal-all (Prunella vulgaris). I'm organizing a science club at school. So far we have nine members.

We're going to do environmental projects, like sponsoring some sort of Earth Day celebration in the spring. We're also going to join up with the National

Committee for the New River (NCNR) for some of its projects. I'm trying to learn more about the effects of dams on the environment. Don't worry, I won't advise you to tear yours down.

Love,

Angelica


A LANDSCAPE HAS THE POWER to change those with open hearts. I became attuned to the Appalachians, perhaps as old as Earth itself. Their permanence added to my sense of stability about myself, the knowledge that for millennia rain and wind continued to wear the rough places smooth, but the mountains survived.

I sensed their shifts in mood. Like full-bosomed grandmothers, they embraced the hiker, the camper. Sometimes dark clouds hovered above, and the mountains became foreboding. They could be playful too, as when the sun appeared and disappeared behind clouds whose shadows danced over treetops swaying in the wind. Or depressed, simply standing there passively, as if waiting for a noteworthy activity to come along.

I absorbed the landscape much as parched earth absorbs rainfall.

My spirit was also fed by the physicality of each day. Burrowing naked hands into the dirt, soil lodging under my fingernails, I contemplated the mysteries of gardening. A small seed dropped in a trench, covered by dirt. Surrounded by darkness and moisture it comes to life. Straw mulch protects it from choking weeds until it begins to produce, sometimes so profusely the gardener can't keep pace.

I came to understand Earth as my partner in this new life of mine.

I was blessed to be welcomed into the circle of women who first visited the store. On summer Sundays we had picnics; in the winter we met in each others' homes. Except for a brief rebellious period in college, I'd obeyed the Brothers' position against alcoholic beverages. Now, in wine's afterglow my shyness lessened. Sometimes I asked myself, is it really me who's laughing so hard? Is it me who feels accepted by these wonderful women?

But sometimes wine had the opposite effect, and conversations turned solemn. I had assumed that I alone carried a burden from the past. But over time, as twilight turned to darkness and the coals of a fire, whether built inside or out-of-doors, turned red, my friends would unbandage their wounds. Everyone present formed an emotional circle of support around whoever shared her sorrow.

Nada Sue told how the year she and her husband both turned forty-two he died of pancreatic cancer, leaving her to raise three teenagers on her own. For a long time she wanted to remarry but never found another man to match him. Now she worried about her daughter, thirty-eight, out in California, who believed that surely one of the movie producers and directors she slept with would fulfill her dreams of becoming a movie actress.

Fran, after being married for twenty-four years and having two children, had come to terms with being a lesbian. Even though she and her former husband had divorced amicably, and her adult children were accepting, she sometimes felt profound loss. She'd lost her church, many of her friends, and her status as a community leader.

Peachie had three times been divorced and remarried. "I'd say 'lucky at cards, unlucky in love,' except every time I go to Cherokee, I lose," she said. Though age had depleted her sexual urgings, she craved cuddling and having someone to talk with over breakfast.

Three times a week Marguerite drove up to Johnson City to spend time with her husband, who had Alzheimer's and was in a nursing home. She sometimes reminisced about earlier times, especially their travel adventures when he'd still been a vibrant man.

Only Amelia offered no clues about the pain she lived with, no explanation for her damaged body. Neither did anyone press her to speak.

For more than a year I hesitated to say much about my own past. What would my friends make of the world I'd come from? Surely they'd laugh, for nothing like the Community of Brothers existed down here. And Wendell? I had no explanation for why I'd left him. But once I started to talk about the Sisters and Brothers, once I described the clothes I wore, the church's belief that wives were to obey their husbands, it was Peachie who in her wise mountain way offered the most comfort.

"Why, Sug-ah, you just got swallowed up. That's what happened to you. Like old Jonah down in the belly of that whale. Hard to breathe down there. No room to move 'round in. But once he got regurgitated—whoo-ee. Wasn't nothing gonna stop him. You just be glad you got out. Just think, you could still be down there. Next thing to Hades, as far as I can tell."

After dinner we usually sang. Fran kept up a background strum on her guitar, bending her head forward to follow a progression of finger picking. Amelia's fiddle usually carried the tune, though it wasn't unusual for her to take off improvising. Marguerite kept the rhythm with two spoons. Grasping them in one hand, she clicked the spoons against each other, tapped them against a knee, lifted them in the air. All done with the gracefulness of a snake charmer.

I didn't know the words to the old mountain songs, but my familiarity with hymns gave me a sense of harmonizing. The more wine we consumed the louder the music got. The sadder too. Songs about loves lost and times with no money. One old song never failed to bring tears to my eyes:

[1]Take me back oh hills I love; Lift me from this lonely bed.
Light my way with stars above; Curl soft winds about my head.
Wash my feet in crystal streams; Cradle my arms in boughs of oak.
Breathe the scent of pine for dreams; Wrap me tight in earthen cloak.

---

[1]"Appalachian Round," published in William Walker'
The Southern Harmony and Musical Companion.

~~~

WE SAT IN WEBBED LAWN CHAIRS near the willow tree by the pond. Atop a makeshift table of boards spread across sawhorses, Cloth of Terra's gold threads glistened in the sun's late afternoon glow. I was hosting a send-off party. On Monday Angelica, after spending the month of August with me, would head back to Virginia and her junior year of high school.

They called her Aunt Mabel, the woman Marguerite and Fran brought along. Whose aunt wasn't at all clear. In her eighties, she was slight in build, her jaws sunken from the loss of teeth.

"Used to come to this neck a the woods as a girl," she said after the meal, while Fran and Amelia tuned their instruments. "Grandpa, he brung me." She made a circular motion that seemed to include the whole farm. "Over yonder hill and…" Her face lit up. "Why I wonder if I could find it."

Bent forward, Fran had her ear close to the guitar. Amelia was running the bow over the strings of her violin. Both looked up to ask simultaneously, "Find what?"

"Mmm, how 'bout we go for a lil hike?" The cane wobbled as Aunt Mabel tried to get up.

Angelica rushed to take an elbow. "Yes, yes!"

This late in the evening? The sun, though not yet resting on the mountains across the valley, had already introduced fuchsia to western clouds. But the musicians were returning their instruments to black cases, and Angelica still stood beside Aunt Mable, her eyes alight with eagerness to follow. I rushed into the house to get a flashlight. Just in case.

I'd never trespassed on the neighbors' land. Not that I had any indication they would object if I walked through their fields. My hikes took me in the opposite direction, up the knoll behind the vacant chicken house, then northeast up to the ridge. Aunt Mabel, though, forged a way among hay bales in the adjacent field, then followed the stream that fed my pond. With surprising speed, the aged woman led us along vestiges of a seldom-used trail. Uphill through touch-me-nots and Joe-Pye weed.

From my place at the end of the line, I observed Angelica walking slightly behind Aunt Mable, sometimes stepping forward to offer her arm for support.
~~~

The group entered the forest, moss-carpeted with clusters of fern. Wrinkled yellow fruit still clung to a few may apples. Wild grape vines, their girth larger than nearby saplings, climbed tulip trees. The charred bark of a hickory tree recently struck by lightening lay scattered around the splintered trunk. Deeper and deeper into wooded darkness the old woman led us. Every now and then the stream was out of sight. Yet we could hear it rushing across rocks. Only the path's occasional steep downhill slope slowed Aunt Mabel's pace, causing her to lean on Angelica.

We'd just come upon a clear view of the stream. It was wider here, its waters rushing around boulders. On the opposite bank, in the crevasses of a jagged wall of rock, grew a miniature tulip tree and clusters of saxifrage, a few still with blossoms.

"Not far now," Aunt Mable said.

I felt increasingly uneasy. Darkness was fast approaching. In spite of the elderly woman's confidence, the search—and for what?—was based on a distant memory.

Aunt Mable stopped abruptly and pointed her cane upward. "Bigger for sure, but not many like it."

The ancient oak tree resembled a swayback woman, belly protruding forward. Like arms, two branches ran parallel to the ground several yards before reaching skyward. Just beyond the tree rhododendron and mountain laurel formed what at first appeared to be an impenetrable wall.

Aunt Mabel began poking at the brush with her cane. "All these laurel slicks growed a plenty, though that was the idea. See if you can get through there."

Angelica picked up a broken limb from the ground and began to poke at the brush. I hung back, still skeptical.

"Here," Angelica and Marguerite called out together. Barely enough light penetrated the rhododendron and laurel to see inside the recess their sticks exposed.

Branches scraped against us as single file we stooped and pushed our way in. The recess opened into a large bower. We gazed upon a low fire pit, its crumbled red bricks scattered about. Nearby lay shards of a jug and skeletons of two barrels. I tripped over a rusted pipe.

"A still?" Fran asked just above a whisper.

"Grandpa's," Aunt Mabel said proudly. She laughed. "Revenuers never did find it."

"Did he own this land?" Peaches asked.

"Lord, no." Again Aunt Mabel laughed. "They never let us kids have none, but folks round here said it was the best hooch in the county."

"Moonshine?" Angelica asked. "Isn't it illegal?"

Aunt Mable chewed her gums. "Some laws—now, girl, don't you go telling nobody I told you this—but some laws ought to be broke."

On the trail back to the house, while making our way in dark shadows, Angelica and Aunt Mable talked the whole way.

"Don't take her words too seriously," I later warned Angelica. "These old mountain folks, Scots-Irish they are. They're known to be—I guess you could say they don't like anyone telling them what to do. They'll stand up to just about anybody, the government included."


Dear Mom,

Thanks for letting me stay a whole month. As you know I enjoyed working in your store. Freezing green beans wasn't great, but I'm glad you'll have plenty of them to eat this winter. Daddy and Randy liked the muscadine jelly I brought back. I didn't tell them we made wine too.

It was fun being with your friends. You're a lot different than you used to be, which I think is good.

School has started. In my history class we're working on oral reports. You may be interested to know that I'm doing mine on Prohibition. I'm going to tell about Aunt Mable showing us a still and about her saying some laws ought to be broken. My new boyfriend, Keith, says his dad was arrested for burning his draft card back in the sixties. I plan to end up saying it's stupid to think you can enforce a law against selling alcohol. I'm sure Daddy won't approve.

By the way, Keith plays clarinet in the band and is
real cute.
I miss you.
Love,
Angelica

"I'M SORRY TO HAVE TO TELL YOU THIS." It was my brother,
Daniel, on the phone. "Daddy passed away. He, uh—he took his
own life."

I cried when I peered into the casket. Wearing his dark
church suit, Daddy appeared smaller, not the formidable
presence I used to fear. Balder too, a fringe of silver hair
surrounding his scalp. Pock marks from adolescent acne
appeared deeper. As when he'd lived, his glasses rested lopsided
on his nose.

*Took his own life.* The coroner's words, my brother's words. A
take-charge action. Don't just wait around for death, seize it.
Committed suicide. A negative word, *committed.* Committed a
crime. Committed a sin. Knowingly doing something wrong.
Took his own life to—

Jesus died for my sins, the Brothers taught me. So easy, when
I was a girl, to conclude that Daddy also suffered because of my
sins. *Please, one smile, just one smile,* I wanted to cry out to the body
in the casket.

Seeing him stretched out on a bed of blue satin, the lines of
sorrow across his brow, I felt compassion for my father. Not a
lot. But some.

WHY DON'T I HAVE pleasant memories from growing up? Surely
if I tried, I'd come up with something. Why does my brain cling
to painful ones? Most of them related to Daddy, over dinner, in
the small dining room where a formica table and four gray vinyl
chairs took up nearly all the space. I asked too many questions
and without considering Daddy's reaction expressed
observations that ran counter to the Brothers' dogma.

One evening—I had to have been eight or nine. Over dinner
I'd been gazing at the picture above Daddy's head, the famous
one of Jesus, where he has auburn highlights in his long wavy

hair, and his blue eyes are serenely focused on a distant object.

"Jesus didn't look like that," I blurted.

"Who says he did?" Daniel asked.

"Well, people act like he did."

"You think you know what he looked like?" Daniel challenged, rolling his eyes.

"Yeah, he was fat and bald." As if my comment wasn't already blasphemous enough, I giggled.

"Elizabeth!" That was my father.

"Maybe not, but in the school library I saw some pictures in *National Geographic* of people who live in the desert, and their hair is all icky. They don't wash it, and the men all need a haircut really bad. Everybody's missing a bunch of teeth. I think Jesus looked like them. He probably had a tooth missing, one right in front."

"Stop it!"

"Eat your supper, Elizabeth," Mama pleaded. "Here, have some more cornbread." She hated it when disagreements arose, especially if they upset Daddy.

But I was intent on making my point. "Think about it. The guy walked in the desert sand and wore sandals."

"We do not speak of our lord as a guy," Daddy thundered. He had a voice to match his size: robust and intimidating. By now his face was beet red and his fists were clenched.

But I was wound up and couldn't have stopped if I'd tried. "Don't you see, we don't really know what he looked like. That robe"—I pointed up at the picture—"it looks like it's just been washed and ironed. Do you think he carried an extra robe with him, a clean one? Why didn't Matthew or Mark say, 'So Jesus packed his suitcase and headed for—for, say Nazareth.' You know he could of been really ugly."

"Elizabeth, please," Mama again pleaded.

"Go to your room!" Daddy boomed. "And don't come out until you've given some thought to how you've desecrated the name of our blessed savior."

Looking down at her lap, Mama kept her fingers busy folding and refolding the pleats of her cotton apron.

"What would Jesus say about your attitude?" Daniel taunted.

"Shut up, smarty pants." I stomped to my bedroom and slammed the door.

I hadn't meant to be irreverent, just wanted to discuss an issue I considered interesting. Why couldn't people say, yes, Elizabeth's right, we don't really know what Jesus looked like. Did they believe that only a clean, handsome Jesus could be holy? Or was it the perfect bit? Jesus was perfect, therefore, he had to have perfect hair, perfect teeth, and be perfectly clean.

Or maybe I *was* bad, just like Daddy's voice made it sound. Maybe it was a sin to say such things about God and Jesus. A good girl would have sat at the table, her back straight, left hand in her lap, and nodded her head ever so delicately. She'd have smiled and quietly eaten her hot dogs and beans and said, *Please pass the catsup,* and *Thank you* and *Yes, it was a lovely day today.*

Stretched out on my bed I closed my eyes, wondering if I should go back to the dining room and apologize. I'm sorry I said that about our blessed savior. Yes, I'd go apologize.

I pushed my elbows against the soft mattress in an effort to get up. A faint scent like a Christmas tree wafted over me. My gaze went to the opposite corner of my bedroom, up where the ceiling and walls met. There I saw a woman's face. She was about my mother's age, not quite forty, with dark skin and black eyes, her head covered with the same pink and gray fabric Mama had used to sew my bedroom curtains. Her eyes glowed like lanterns, brightening the room. At the same time they mirrored my sadness and regret.

"You're not bad, Elizabeth," she said. "Believe me, you're not. You're lively and curious, the way a girl should be."

I didn't say a word, just stayed in that position, my head and torso raised, staring at the ceiling, staring at the face so I'd be sure to remember its features.

"I understand you, Elizabeth. Nobody appreciates your liveliness and curiosity, but I do. I love you as my own."

And she was gone.

I can't explain why, but there was no doubt in my mind that I had seen the mother of Jesus. I couldn't measure up to Daddy's expectations, but Mary thought I was worthy of love, not even minding that I had said disrespectful things about her son.

That was the first time she appeared to me.

# Chapter 11

**ROME**

MORE NEWS ELIZABETH'S BEEN FEARING: a CNN report from a mountaintop removal site in West Virginia. Tires on trucks, slashed. Cabs of trucks, burned out. A Caterpillar D9, weighing in the neighborhood of forty-nine tons—someone started it and ran it over the rim. A twenty-story-high dragline, its giant scoop capable of digging tons of earth, was turned on its side. Engine parts she's never heard of were filled with corrosives and substances that gum up the works.

She stands close to the TV, listening for who's responsible. The FBI is investigating. *Oh, my dear daughter! Please, please have nothing to do with this. They'll hunt you down, kill you, not caring that you are a remarkable human being with so much potential for doing good. Certainly not caring that you are loved. You can't stand up to a major coal company and expect it to back down, especially after you've destroyed its trucks and draglines.*

A helicopter flies over the site, the newswoman on board deplores the destruction of equipment. Destruction of equipment? What about the mountain? God's breast severed, leaving a huge quarry, layers of soil blasted away. Rushing streams diverted by the debris. Between the lush forest at the base of the mountain and the gaping hole at the top, fallen trees are scattered like pick-up sticks. *I'm sorry, Ms. Newslady, but I cannot join your lament over the destruction of equipment.*

*Mother Mary, keep Angelica safe.*

To: wl83@torbox3.onion                Sept 28 7:04 AM
Subject: Hi
Dear One,

I must tell you about last night's dream. You were up in the trees. I was there with you, looking way down, yelling at a guy with a chain saw that if that beautiful redwood went down, I'd go with it. I woke up exhilarated. The dream's meaning? I think it's about how much I share your love for the natural world. I want your kind of courage. At the same time I wish you didn't have it. Try making sense of that!

In spite of one energizing dream, my thoughts about you are filled with anxiety. When Mary Surratt intrudes in my thoughts, with all her talk about love of land and the justice of her cause, it's you, not her, I see hanging from a rope.

There's been no sign here of the other Mary. My search, though, has allowed me an unexpected blessing. While the Brothers reject decoration in the sanctuary, here I've become connected to art, its ability to capture emotion and beauty. Every day I stand in awe of the power of paint upon canvas.

Please stay safe.

Love,
Mom


IN SANTA MARIA IN VALLICELLA, before an enormous canvas, Elizabeth feels an almost overwhelming anticipation. There is familiarity in this Blessed Mother-to-be. Mary and her pregnant cousin (also named Elizabeth) reach out to each other in a half-embrace, clasping shoulders and hands. They are of peasant stock, far from the halls of power, with no reason to believe the babes in their wombs will ever influence the world beyond. Yet any moment now the two will sing a prayer of hope, that God will use their sons to return the land to the Jews, that the Romans and their collaborators will be sent away empty-handed.

Elizabeth whispers, "Surely you knew your sons' actions would result in death."

SO FAR SHE'S FOCUSED her attention on churches, heaving open weathered wooden doors, some plain, some with biblical scenes intricately carved on them. Inside, rows of arches separate naves from side aisles; vaulted roofs supported by thick granite columns reach heavenward. Walls insulate interiors from outside temperatures, and stained glass windows filter the light of day. There are echoes of shoes landing on concrete, Bibles and prayer books being closed. Sometimes images of Mary are prominent; at other times they're hidden in dark chapels off to the side or in alcoves.

After exploring walls and alcoves, peering intently at statues, wood carvings, painted canvases, Elizabeth often sits in a pew toward the back of a nave. She lifts jumbled and contradictory prayers. Gratitude for Angelica's moral outrage and courage. Appeals that for the sake of the planet the group will succeed. That they won't succeed, and some benign interference will give Angelica no alternative but to return to her studies. *Keep her safe, keep her safe, keep her safe.*

Prayers on Elizabeth's own behalf follow: *I've lived my three score. It is my life that should be put on the line, not Angelica's. Free me from fear and doubt. Give me a dose of her courage.*

And Mary? What did she pray, Elizabeth often wonders. *Please, God, help my son and his band succeed, so that our land is returned to us. Please tell him to give up the mission and return to his father's business as a craftsman. Keep him safe, keep him safe, keep him safe.*

SMARTLY DRESSED ITALIAN WOMAN walk by the outdoor café where Elizabeth takes the last swallow from a glass of wine. Some of the women carry briefcases and loaves of bread, others hold the hands of dark haired children with expressive brown eyes. The stalls of a few flower vendors remain open this late in the day.

Tourists with Frommers or Rick Steves guidebooks underarm stop to aim cameras at the statue of Dominican Friar Bruno Giordano, burned alive here in 1600 for heresy, according to Elizabeth's travel book. Ecclesiastical authorities denounced his belief that the earth orbits the sun. Giordano didn't help his cause by also doubting that Mary was a virgin.

Behind Elizabeth's chair a wall plaque proclaims the excellent quality of the proprietor's wine and displays a laughing Bacchus in bas-relief. She agrees, it is good wine. But all she's eaten today have been two rolls smeared with butter and some yogurt, and as she waits for her order of gnocchi, she imagines her drunken self leaning in the chair until her head lands in the lap of the young man at the next table having a beer with friends.

It's been a day characterized mainly by futility. Entering churches, turning her pocket flashlight on each dark nook. She's counted the Marys: thirty-six today. They've all stayed stuck to the canvas or on pedestals, expressions unchanging.

The gnocchi arrives, a salad after that. She finishes them and orders another glass of wine. Salu, she says, smiling and lifting the glass in the direction of the young men. They smile and lift their glasses as well. Just as she's about to return her gaze to passersby, something in her peripheral vision catches her attention. She turns to look up at the plaque. Instead of Bacchus, her father grins down at her.

Her first thought is that she's looking at the kind of cartoon pictures that used to appear in the children's pages of the church magazine, the kind where you look at it one way and it's a bald man frowning, then you turn it around and the bald head is a chin, and the man's smiling. The message: turn your frown into a smile.

"I've been thinking," Vernon says, "I'd like to see the Pantheon."

She turns away from the plaque and concentrates on her glass of wine. He keeps talking. "You know, I'm fascinated by the idea of changing a temple to the gods into a church. And how the dome looks like an eye from the inside. Did you know Raphael's buried there?"

Rotating so that her back is to the table of men (their conversation made noisier by multiple rounds of beer), she tries to speak to Vernon without anyone noticing.

"You, the joy-god?"

"Some of the time. There are things about Bacchus you probably don't know. After the vines bear grapes, the pruner comes along and cuts them back to where there's only a stalk. Until spring everything looks pretty much dead. Bacchus doesn't laugh during the winter, did you know that? He understands the cycles of life and—"

"I don't need a lesson in vine maintenance or mythology. I want to know why you never showed me that smile when I was growing up. Being around so much sadness couldn't help but make me sad too."

"It may sound strange, but when I was living I was dead, and now that I'm dead I can live."

"Meaning what?"

"Guess you could say I got my seasons confused."

# Chapter 12

Dear Mom,

I'm writing to ask if I can come live with you. I'm tired of living with two men. They do nothing to keep the house clean and think I'm the only one qualified to do any inside work.

The main reason I want to move is so I can attend the University of North Carolina after I graduate. They have a good biology department, which is what I want to major in. Once there, I'll find a specialty where I can make the biggest contribution. If I live with you and establish residency I can pay instate tuition.

Please say yes, Mom. I promise I'll help you with the store and the garden. Just don't make me pick up your underwear and socks (like Daddy and Randy do).

Love,
Angelica

Mid-August Angelica moved her collections of rocks and insect casings, her nature books, trombone, and clothes down to North Carolina. By October she'd already made first-chair trombone in the high school band and had a boyfriend. On weekends she helped stock the shelves of the store and, until the first heavy frost, worked in the garden.

I marveled that this slender, auburn-haired beauty was my daughter, a girl on the cusp of womanhood yet still exuding a child's enthusiasm for life. She was everything I hadn't been at that age. By then I'd dutifully ceased questioning my father, the church, and God. My future self, when I contemplated the years ahead, faced nothing beyond a preordained world: the Community of Brothers and wifedom. I never considered the possibility of dreams, never gave thought to having a lasting impact beyond my family.

Sundays Angelica and I often climbed over the fence marking the boundary between farm and state land to make our way up the forested mountain. Jezebel, nose to the ground, led us. Sometimes we hiked without speaking, the silence broken by snapping twigs and dry fall leaves crunching beneath our boots. Sometimes we talked about school, current events, the store.

Upon reaching the crest, we would follow the trail to a table-top boulder in a clearing bordered by aged rhododendron, their leggy trunks coated in gray lichen. On the boulder's southern face, we ate a picnic lunch, usually cheese or peanut butter sandwiches and an apple. Afterwards, elbows resting against raised knees, we sipped from thermos cups—hot tea in Angelica's, coffee in mine—and looked out over the bowl-shaped valley below, beyond it ridge after ridge after ridge.

Photographs on the walls of the local general store showed this area in the 1910s, when as far as the eye could see there were only jagged tree stumps. Virgin forest had survived the millennia only to lose to the logging industry. Now forests hosted trees with slender trunks, all stretching skyward, competing for light.

Shortened winter days didn't bring an end to our Sunday hikes. We followed trails among leafless trees, their gray nakedness revealing twisted trunks and intersecting branches. Here and there a cluster of evergreens interrupted the bleakness: flat-needled hemlocks, scruffy spruce pines, and white pines.

In the distance we could hear the low of a cow or the grind of a car engine climbing a steep grade.

THE STORE WAS DRAWING customers from a wider area, generating more work than I could handle. Some weekends Angelica helped, but band and the school newspaper dominated any free time she might have had.

As much as I enjoyed baking, I hired Millie Henshaw to make the homemade cakes, pies, and cookies. Nada Sue came up with another idea. A lot of young people wanted to learn the basics of organic gardening and marketing. What if I took on apprentices? I could offer housing, food, and experiential education in exchange for labor.

Before long the pounding of a hammer and the high-pitched whine of a table saw interrupted the valley quiet. Hank Lavernik was transforming the former chicken house into a cozy cabin, upgrading it with insulation, wall boarding, vinyl flooring, indoor plumbing, and kitchen cabinets.

EVEN WITH THE WINDOWS OPEN, the acrid odor of vinegar overpowered the senses. Every now and then I stuck my head out the door, took a deep breath, and inhaled the fresh mountain air.

Two summer interns from South Carolina were due to arrive the following week, and a drinking binge had put Hank behind schedule. Instead of going to a movie with friends on a Friday night, Angelica was helping me get the cabin ready. While I collected wood scraps and other debris Hank had left scattered around, she worked in the alcove kitchen, spraying a brew of vinegar, baking soda, and water on the interior of a small refrigerator. If we couldn't get rid of the mold inside, it wouldn't even be worth the four dollars Hank had paid at the Monday night auction.

Angelica applied extra pressure to traces of greenish-gray. "I can't stand Todd McConnell," she said between grunts. "Today—this is what I mean. In history class we've been studying the Industrial Revolution. Mr. Walsh got us talking about the Unabomber, what he wrote in his manifesto about the Industrial Revolution. He said it was a disaster for the human race."

She stood from her squatting position and stretched. Wendell wouldn't have approved of her tight jeans and the faded Camp Covenant t-shirt accentuating her breasts.

"Mr. Walsh wanted to know if we agree or disagree. So Todd—he's such an asshole. Excuse me, Mom, but he really is. He starts talking about how he wouldn't have his great Mustang if it wasn't for the Industrial Revolution, and no Ted Krazy-inski—that's what he calls him—is going to take away his car.

Then he says anybody who agrees with Krazy-inski is as loony as he is."

She stepped back to admire her effort. Satisfied that the interior was clean, she plugged the refrigerator in. At the sound of its monotone hum, she clapped her hands.

"I don't—there's something about him." She next began unpacking a box of plates and glasses, stretching to place them in a shallow cabinet over the sink "I wish I could keep my big mouth shut. So I say, 'Kaczynski's right, technology *is* the enemy. Every time you drive your precious Mustang you're producing carbon dioxide, which gets trapped in the atmosphere, and it's heating the planet.'

"Then I started arguing how electricity's doing the same thing, the demand for it, and Todd's saying if I don't like refrigerators and electric lights I can go live like Krazy-inski, and he's got all the kids laughing." She wiped tears from her cheek with the sleeve of her t-shirt. "And I say the Unabomber was trying—that we all should stand up for our convictions."

"And your teacher. Didn't he intervene?"

"Not really. He said—to me he's saying this—'So what if everyone who believes society's going in the wrong direction, what if they mailed bombs to people they think are responsible?' And I said—I said, 'How else do you get people's attention?'" She stepped over to me and wrapped her vinegar-smelling arms around my neck. "Mom, sometimes I think I'm the only one who gives a damn."

"I care. I care too." But not nearly as much as Angelica did.

The passion I caught glimpses of now and then frightened me.


I MANEUVERED FORESTED MOUNTAIN ROADS, slowing at times to take S-curves that followed the river, speeding up on straight-aways. Jezebel sat on her haunches in the truck bed, facing into the wind, eyes closed in bliss. Angelica rode with the window open, arm propped on the door frame, inhaling the scents of budding trees and mossy woods.

"Actually I don't think Kaczynski's crazy," she said. "Someone's got to protect all this."

As if following a downhill slope on skis, I leaned into a series of curves. Steering to the left. To the right. Thinking about *crazy*; who is, who isn't; who gets to define it.

I didn't intend to speak out loud. "Sometimes I think I'm crazy." There they were, words of truth blurted into the ether.

"Huh?"

"Uh, you know, the way I live, the way I look." I tugged at the bib of my overalls, hoping the gesture would suggest a crazy woman's choice of attire.

"I don't think you are."

To our right the river narrowed, rushing riotously over rocks.

"Would it matter to you if I were?" I asked.

She continued to peer out the window. "You're not." After a few seconds of quiet, she reached over to touch my arm. "You're not talking about clothes, though, are you, Mom?"

Decades before, when no older than Angelica, I'd successfully pushed Mary away. But I was a grown woman now, and since I'd moved down to North Carolina, Mary had again appeared. Leaving me confused about reality.

There was something about my daughter, about this moment. A significance. It was an occasion for honesty.

"Voices," I said. "I used to—well, sometimes I still—I hear voices. Not often, just once in awhile. Mary, for one. The mother of Jesus—she first appeared to me when I was, oh, probably nine or ten."

"You mean…the…you mean the Virgin Mary?"

A faint laugh. "A virgin? Lord, no. But, yes, the one you're thinking about. She helped me survive childhood. Daddy was all the—well, you knew your grandfather."

"It was obvious you two had issues. The time—it meant a lot, you standing up for me that time they were visiting and I announced I was going to be a vegetarian. Grandpa quoted scripture—something about meat—and you defended me. I never told you that, how much it meant."

I reached across, patted her leg, and smiled.

"Blasphemy," I said, "that's what he called my questions when I was a kid. 'To your room!' he'd yell and point his finger like I didn't know the way. I didn't mind though, because

Mary—she'd be up there in the corner of my bedroom ceiling. She told me I was a good girl and that I was smart, like her daughters. I needed to hear that, that I was all right."

I took my eyes off the road to see Angelica's reaction. Wanting her to know the truth, at the same time wondering whether I was describing reality or hallucinations. "Wish I had a dollar for every time I was sent from the table without supper."

"For one. You said, the Vir-Blessed Mother, *for one*."

Had I said *for one*? Well… "A woman named Mary Surratt too. She sort of pops in and out of my consciousness. Not often. She was hanged for the assassination of Lincoln."

"Didn't John Wilkes Booth—?"

"She was part of the conspiracy. One summer our family took a trip to Washington D.C. I got a brochure at Ford's Theater." All glossy and smooth, I still remembered, with a picture of Mary Surratt on the front. "I don't know how many hours I spent reading it, staring at her picture. She promised to be my friend and tell me secrets. I didn't have many friends."

I braked as we came to a sharp curve. "When I wrote my eighth grade history report about her, I got a D. The teacher said I made it all up. I didn't. Mary S. told me everything."

"Wow." Silence. "So does she come—is it like a nightmare?"

"No, she talks to me during the day. Not often, just once in a while. It's kind of like scraping scabs with a fingernail. I just have to listen to her relive her final days. I don't know whether that's her hell to pay, or—or—there've been others, other voices. Not many."

In case all this frightened Angelica, I added, "Mostly when I was young, not so much anymore."

A yellow road sign with a black squiggly line and a downhill grade caused me to brake again. For a time I concentrated on driving, turning the steering wheel left then right then left, then right again.

"She's come back twice since I moved down here."

"Mary Surratt or the Vir—the other Mary?"

"The holy Mary. I'd been here less than a week. Out of the blue, there she stands, out by the stoop. There'd been no sign of her since I was—I was about fourteen, I think. She's come once more."

"Kind of like a lover who sneaks in when nobody else is around?"

"And just what do you know of lovers who sneak in?"

"I read books, you know."

We heard its roar before we saw it. Coming out of a sharp curve we came up on what all winter long had been a trickle, now a cascade. "Oooo," we said simultaneously. I pulled into a small gravel parking area beside the road and turned off the engine. No more than a hundred yards away, water plummeted down a giant's stair steps, thundering where it crashed into boulders, separating into divergent streams where rocks blocked its passage. Beyond, trickles and swiftly flowing branches merged, joining to feed a pool at the bottom. On both sides of the falls, trees with fisted spring-green leaves played with sprays of water, creating mottled patterns of light. It was a scene of such profound beauty that for a while neither of us said anything.

Angelica cleared her throat and spoke so quietly that I could hardly understand her against the clamor. "I kind of hear voices too. It's not hearing as much as—like right now, the waterfalls and my blood—it's like they're mixed, flowing together through my arteries. Sounds crazy, doesn't it?" With both hands she wiped tears from the corners of her eyes.

"No crazier than your mother hearing dead people."

"In Sunday school we memorized the twenty-third Psalm. When I recited it to get that little bookmark Sister Petry gave out, I cried when I got to 'He maketh me to lie down in green pastures, he leadeth me beside the still waters.' I never told you that, did I?"

"No, but it doesn't surprise me."

"If I was writing my own psalm I'd say something like, my soul is in the sap of the tree, in the pollen of a daisy. It rides the back of a fleeting red fox."

She quit speaking. The only sound beyond the pickup truck was water pounding against rocks. I put both hands on the steering wheel and leaned into it, eyes closed. As if by doing so I might capture this precious moment with my daughter.

Angelica spoke. "I wonder—sometimes I look at something like this waterfall and the views we come across when we hike, and I imagine the indigenous people. I wonder what it was like to see this for the first time. No road. They're just walking along, hunting maybe, and they come to this. Did they go *wow*, or was natural beauty so ordinary they didn't think much about it?"

I lifted my head from the steering wheel. "They sang songs to Mother Moon. Honoring Earth, its bounty, it was part of their religion. Yes, I think Earth's beauty spoke to them. Like it speaks to you."

"Like the Marys speak to you?"

"Maybe. Maybe."

Angelica leaned across the seat to kiss me on the cheek. "I don't think either of us is crazy. Just—how about unique?"

# Chapter 13

THE PUNGENT SCENT OF LEMON-GINGER tea hovered in the air as I filled two pottery mugs. Angelica sat at the round kitchen table, a stack of school books to her left, pencil moving rapidly across a sheet of lined paper. A pause, a hasty erasure, more writing.

I placed a mug beside her and pulled out a chair. "I'm thinking about changing my last name."

She finished writing a thought, put down her pencil, and looked up. "Change your name?"

"I've decided I don't want your father's name."

Angelica watched the swirl of the honey stick over her tea. "'What's in a name? That which we call a rose by any other name would smell as sweet.' Elizabeth Mattison, Elizabeth Jones, Elizabeth Jingle-Heimerschmidt. Thinking about going back to Pierson?"

I dismissively waved my hand. "No, I don't want my father's name either."

She sat up straight, eyes bright with mock enthusiasm. "How about Garbo? Curie, Barton. Hey, this offers all kinds of creative possibilities."

"Don't make light of it. I'm serious. I want a name with significance."

"What kind of significance?"

"I keep trying to think of someone who made a difference, a name that's been forgotten." A trace of laughter. "But then if it's forgotten I won't be able to remember it. A woman. They're usually forgotten."

"Thinking literature? History? Science?"

"Sorry, I guess I brought you into this prematurely. Go back to your homework."

~~~
~~~

"WHAT'S IN A NAME?" Juliet asked.

By the time I was born Daddy's sisters had taken most of the good female Bible names: Esther, Ruth, Naomi, Rachael, Hannah, and Rebecca. He decided on Elizabeth and made it clear no one was to call me Liz or Lizzy.

Reading *Little Women* I identified with Beth and imagined myself a one-syllable-type personality. There was, of course, a major downside to identifying with her. She died. I'd remind myself to be Bethlike: meek, unselfish, pure. She had no goals other than to please her parents. She showed no signs of curiosity and never questioned Holy Scripture as I was prone to do. Daddy would surely love me more if I were like her.

I finally got up the nerve to tell him and Mama, "From now on I want to be called Beth."

"Elizabeth," Daddy insisted.

How brash to name an infant before we even know her. Assuming she'll grow to fit the name. Wendell's and my choice for what to call our daughter? It was a spur-of the-moment decision, made within hours of her birth. We looked down into the sweet face of the blanket-wrapped infant in my arms and agreed she looked like an angel.

But Angelica wasn't the one searching for a new name. She seemed satisfied. And over the years I had resigned myself to being Elizabeth.

My family name, though, seemed more significant. It implied connection. Like the Kennedy clan and the Roosevelts. I didn't want to be connected to the Mattisons or Piersons.

Peaches, one time when our group was discussing Latin America, referred to the concept of *accompaniment.* That was what I wanted: a new last name that signaled my desire to accompany.


"MCNAIR," I SAID WHILE ANGELICA and I cleaned the kitchen after dinner. "I've decided to go by Elizabeth McNair."

She scraped potato peelings and apple stems into the compost jar. "Where'd that come from?"

"Denise McNair. One of four little girls killed in the Birmingham church bombing back in 1963. For a long time after

I saw her picture I thought about how I had my whole life ahead of me, and she might have had hers too. Only she didn't."

"So you're thinking—?"

"Her mother, Mrs. McNair—even after all these years she's probably still living with the *ifs*. If we'd just skipped church that morning. Overslept or read the paper over a leisurely breakfast. If we'd moved up North like we considered. The rest of us—our lives, they went on. But this woman, she's probably still mourning." I heaved a deep sigh. "It's a way for me to accompany a grieving mother."

McNair it was.

MAMA PULLED HER SUITCASE into the waiting area of the Asheville airport. Even after she looked around, spotted Angelica and me, and cheerfully waved, she continued an animated conversation with a well dressed middle-aged man carrying a briefcase.

This was my mother? Speaking like an old friend with a man outside the Community of Brothers? A stranger? And her clothes. Not a plain cotton dress with bibbed bodice, which she'd worn as long as Daddy was alive, but bright blue pants and a white corduroy blazer. I would soon discover that her suitcase contained, in addition to jeans and cotton pants (all with elastic waists), three sweatshirts: one with teddy bears and sequins, another with fish and sequins, the third with flowers and sequins. She still wore her hair gathered in a bun at the nape of her neck.

Instead of staying one week, as planned, she stayed five. At her request I moved a rocking chair from inside the house to the small hospitality table in the store, where she served iced mint tea and engaged in friendly chatter with customers. When not playing hostess, she could be found on the living room sofa watching *General Hospital* or *Guiding Light*. Daddy had never allowed a television set in the house. It was *of* the world.

I waited for Mama to criticize me for wearing my hair like a man, for not going to church, for spending Sunday evenings with my friends drinking wine and singing. Instead she expressed no disapproval, even joined in song on Sunday evenings, sipping apple juice as she harmonized in a smooth alto voice.

Yet the visit wasn't without conflict.

I had worked in the store all day. Mama and Angelica had cleaned and packaged fresh lettuce from the garden. Now the three of us ate dinner at the picnic table on the patio. Though a breeze wafted from the south, the May air was still chilly. Angelica wore a faded University of North Carolina sweatshirt; Mama wore the sweatshirt with teddy bears and sequins across the front. I had on a bulky wool sweater I'd found at Alice's Closet, a second-hand clothing store.

Near the patio two pale pink azalea bushes bloomed and the dogwood boasted its white cross-shaped blossoms. In the garden beyond, beets were up, their red and green leaves branching out. Peas were forming on vines.

"What's on TV tonight?" Mama asked. She took a bite of the tofu burger drowned in catsup and winced. Several days earlier, on a trip into Mars Hill, she'd requested a stop at McDonald's to buy a hamburger.

"Don't know," Angelica said. "I've got a science paper to finish."

"What's it about?"

Angelica's body stiffened. She looked directly into her grandmother's eyes. "Actually it's about your generation, the way you abused the environment. You assumed there were unlimited resources." She motioned toward the large glass bowl just out of reach. "I'll take some more spinach salad, please…. Let industries dump their chemicals in the water. All in the name of progress. So now my generation, we're left to clean it all up."

Mama set down her fork and brought both hands to her chest. Behind clear glasses frames, her eyes started to water.

With the certainty of adolescence, Angelica continued. "Plastic, you liked plastic. It doesn't break, well not so—"

"That's enough." I didn't often exercise parental authority, but I reached over and grasped Angelica's wrist. "You can't blame your grandmother—"

"I don't mean it personally."

"Well, it certainly sounds—"

Mama rose from the picnic table. "Can I get anyone some more iced tea?"

"Thanks, Mama. Nothing for me."

As the screen door slammed behind her, Angelica whispered, "Proves my point, her leaving at just this minute. She doesn't want to hear the truth."

"You're not going to get anywhere by attacking people."

"But I want her to see that it's her generation that messed things up. They're responsible for the crisis the earth's in."

"No more than your generation. Or mine. I'm afraid, Darling, that you're not typical for your age group. That boy with the Mustang, for instance."

"Well, I'm not going to just sit around waiting for people to see what happens." She left the table and stomped down the hill toward the pond, Jezebel at her heels, leaving me alone at the picnic table.

Again the screen door slammed. Carrying her glass of iced tea, Mama looked around. "Goodness gracious, what got into that girl?"

"I'm sorry she lashed out at you. I wish I could look into the future and see what in the world she's going to do with all that passion."

# Chapter 14

WHENEVER ANYONE ASKED how Angelica was doing—which customers seldom failed to do—I couldn't help but stand a little taller. During her four years at the University of North Carolina she'd matured into a competent young woman. She had a wide circle of friends, dated nice boys, made good grades. After graduation in late May she'd fly to Oregon to spend the summer *in the field*, collecting water samples and peering at them under a microscope. In the fall she would begin her studies in environmental sciences at Duke. Her long-term goal was to earn a doctorate.

How could I not feel proud of my daughter?

*WILLOW POND NATURAL FOODS* was printed in green on both sides of my new white pickup truck. In Asheville I planned to see my accountant and stop by the Gravely dealership to look at new tractors. Buy seed potatoes, some garden tools. And search for a graduation present for Angelica.

At around two in the afternoon I exited the hardware store with two expandable fishnet shopping bags hanging from my right arm. In my left hand a hoe and rake banged against each other as I awkwardly walked toward the truck.

Without warning, gravity released me. With the lightness of a balloon, I felt myself being lifted from the ground, carried higher and higher. I tried holding on to the tools and bags, until I had no choice but to let go. I stretched out my hands, trying to touch, stretching further, trying harder to touch whatever was carrying me upward.

The smell. The Christmas-tree fragrance of the candle I bought as a girl at Holy Name Gift Shop.

"Mary?"

She stood before me, suspended in air. She carried a worn leather satchel. "Elizabeth, the time has come. It may even be too late. We dare not postpone the mission."

"Mission?" Through my mental fog I pictured the Sunday school class of my girlhood, when a piggy bank was passed around and children put in nickels and dimes. "Food for?—Sister Miller said it was for children of heathen nations."

"We're talking about catastrophe on a global scale. You've got to help me rescue Earth."

I laughed. "Now wait a minute. We've hardly had any contact for more than thirty years. You only know Elizabeth the girl, not Elizabeth the woman. And now you've got some—"

"Earth is in crisis. To accompany her through these difficult times we must change human activity. First we'll invite women to your farm."

"Women? What women?"

"A bunch. From anywhere."

"Why? Why my farm?"

"Humanity must turn from its ways. Only women can make that happen."

"Huh? So where will they all sit? I only have six kitchen chairs."

"Outside, on the ground. They'll eat there too, and spend the night."

"But I only have one bathroom."

"We'll bring in port-a-potties."

"Women hate port-a-potties. They stink."

"I can handle that."

"Eat? Spend the night? Who's going to fix the food? Where will they sleep?"

"We'll set up tents."

"And when they get up in the morning? They've got to take showers. What about hair dryers? They've got to have a place to plug in hair dryers."

"E-liz-a-beth trust me. We'll work out the logistics."

"I'm just a farmer. And a store owner. You can't expect me—what you're talking about takes—"

"I once asked the same kinds of questions." Mary faded from sight.

The cement sidewalk pressed hard against my back. I opened my eyes. A man was grasping my wrist as several hushed people crowded around.

"Let them through," someone shouted. The crowd separated and the man released his hold. "Amazing that she came to," he said. "Her heart's only beating at twenty-seven beats a minute."

"I'm all right," I whispered as paramedics lifted me onto a stretcher. "Really, I'm all right."

Someone placed a blanket over me. The next thing I knew I was being hooked up to machines and the ambulance siren was blaring.

"I'm fine," I insisted at the hospital while doctors probed. "I'm fine," I said as nurses drew samples of blood.

"In my professional opinion, you need to be held for observation," said a white-clad woman appearing to be of high school age, *Dr.* on her name tag. Soon a man in blue was wheeling me from the emergency room to the elevator, up to the hospital's third floor.

Not long after midnight, when only a skeleton staff remained on duty, I disconnected the apparatuses. I put on my clothes, peered both directions from the door of my room, and tiptoed out. All was eerily quiet. To avoid the nurses' station, I descended the stairs at the opposite end of the hall.

Me, of all people, called to embark on—it sounded like a crucial mission—personally appointed by Mary. Rescuing Earth? Not from aliens. Nor from a dictator. In any case, I wasn't going to waste time in a hospital.

OUT IN THE GARDEN Jezebel whimpered and paced. I looked up from the row of hills where I was planting potato eyes. A short distance away, Mary, hand held up to shield her eyes from the sun, stood with feet apart. She wore a wind-breaker over loose trousers and kameez. Earmuffs too. Her shoulders were slumped, her head drooped.

Leaving the hoe and burlap bag of potato eyes on the ground, I stepped across the furrow to meet her. No words passed between us as I took her by the arm, helping her navigate the corrugated ridges of the plowed garden.

Mary stopped abruptly. "All this is sacred," she said, the sweep of her arm indicating the entire landscape. "The spirits of native people, they're still present, and you are their guest."

"Yes, I am aware of that." Often, when I saw shadows silently sweep across the landscape, I assumed them to be past dwellers.

We continued walking toward the house, Mary leaning on my arm.

"The land. Ours was sacred too. Those stories Yeshu told—vineyards and harvests." She stumbled. I held on to her. "The crowds, they knew what he was talking about. When your land's been stolen and you're left with nothing—it's freezing out here."

"Your jacket's not heavy enough. Where'd you come from anyway?"

"Bangladesh. That's why I—I'll get to that."

At the back stoop I squatted to remove our muddy shoes. We entered the house in stocking feet. Jezebel ran under the kitchen table, where she lay whimpering.

During the months of winter and early spring, the kitchen and living room had been closed off from the rest of the house. The upstairs was cold, but the wood burning stove kept the living area as cozy as I imagined Mama Bear's winter den.

"I can't seem to get warm," Mary said, rubbing her hands together in front of the stove. I lifted the crocheted granny-square afghan from the back of the sofa to wrap around her shoulders.

"Stay here by the fire. I'll go make some hot tea."

As a young girl, while I still paid attention to the voices, I had maintained a two-realm system of sorts. The world of home, school, and church—I knew that one was real. The second realm, I wasn't sure of: the ethereal—though I didn't know the word *ethereal*—where Mary and an occasional apparition dwelled—though I didn't know the word *apparition* either. Mama and Mother Mary never occupied the same realm. In the kitchen, as I took mugs from the cupboard and placed loose tea in a ceramic pot, the boundaries of the realms blurred.

During my mother's most recent visit, I had become aware that like expiration dates on store products, human shelf life doesn't last forever. Mama, now depending on a cane, was no longer able to flutter around the house singing "Blessed Assurance," or spend hours playing hostess in the store. She'd become an older woman, a slower woman who required patience and different expectations. In a reversal of roles I, the daughter, had become the parent.

In the same manner I had assumed Mary would remain the woman who years ago had appeared in the corner of my bedroom ceiling. That she now seemed fragile puzzled me.

I returned to the living room balancing a tray holding a teapot, two mugs, and a plate of oatmeal cookies. From the cast-iron kettle on the wood-burning stove I poured hot water into the pot. When the tea had steeped long enough, I handed the warm cup to Mary, who continued to stand in front of the stove, the afghan enveloping her.

"I'm sorry I startled you last week," she said, clasping the cup in both hands. She flipped her wrist as a signal of dismissal. "Forget what I said, though. I've changed my mind. That's what I came to tell you. In case you've been wondering."

I took a seat on the nearby sofa and tucked my feet under me. "Sure I've been wondering. A woman doesn't get zapped on a city sidewalk, end up in the hospital, then quickly erase it all from her mind."

"Well, there is something to be said for trying the supernatural approach. A sure way to get attention, that's what Yeshu used to say."

"Something about inviting women, uh, and port-a-potties."

Mary placed her mug and cookie on the small end table. She dropped into the recliner next to it and pulled the handle that raised the footrest.

"Maybe this is how I should spend eternity. Relaxing. Going out for walks, enjoying nature while it lasts." From her baggy pants she withdrew a handkerchief, dabbed at her eyes, and blew her nose. "Rest on my laurels, that's what I'll do, just bask in all the praise for simply giving birth to a baby." She sighed.

"This doesn't sound like the Mary I used to know. You were so upbeat. My personal cheerleader. Go, Elizabeth, go." A faint smile came to her lips. For only a second.

"That was in the past. I'm afraid now it's 'All hope abandon ye who enter here.' Dante's words, of course. Wars, slavery, genocide, I've accompanied the oppressed, the many who suffer. Now my beloved Earth is on the way to becoming Hell." The words spewed from her lips: "Forests turned into malls. Earth's viscera ripped out for her coal, her oil, her uranium."

She closed her eyes and remained silent. Behind the isinglass panel of the stove door an orange-blue flame leaped upward, accompanied by a chorus of crackles and hisses. From the sofa I studied her: the worry lines across her brow, the pinching of her lips. Twice her body jerked.

I left the sofa to sit on the floor next to the recliner. Slowly, tenderly, I began to massage Mary's feet.

"You had some kind of plan you wanted me to be part of."

"That was last week. Before I went to Bangladesh. Yeshu, it angered him the way the poor suffered at the hands of the rich. He could not have imagined. He could not have imagined."

"You mean the poverty there?"

She opened her eyes and leaned forward. "The land. It's always about land. Warming ocean waters are stealing theirs. The poor, that's who pay the… I dropped by to tell you to ignore what I said last week. It's too late."

"Come on, tell me what you had in mind."

"A waste of time. Yours and mine."

"Do you mean telling me is a waste of time, or doing whatever it was you planned?"

"Both." Her jaw was clenched, her eyes set on the wall opposite the recliner.

I stopped the massage and sat back on my haunches. "I won't accept that. They were always about hope, your visits. From the time you first appeared on my bedroom ceiling." I folded my arms across my chest. "Now, tell me your plan. I insist."

At first she pressed her lips together in a gesture of refusal. She took several sips of tea, finished an oatmeal cookie, and started on a second. "All right….I had this crazy notion—I thought women might be able to…to make a difference."

"Meaning what?"

"I was going to call it…" Her jaw quivered as if she were on the verge of tears. "I was going to call it Project: Earth Rescue. A silly idea. Futile. May I have another cookie? I haven't eaten much lately."

"Let me fix you a sandwich. Relax, close your eyes again."

In the kitchen I spread hummus on freshly baked whole wheat bread. "Project: Earth Rescue, Project: Earth Rescue," I repeated over and over.

Returning to the living room I placed the sandwich plate beside the tea cup on the end table. "Get a little food in you, that'll lift your spirits." I opened the door of the stove, poked the two sizzling logs, than waited silently as Mary bit into the sandwich. "Now," I said while replenishing the tea in both cups, "tell me about this idea, the one you've rejected."

Mary chewed and swallowed, chewed and swallowed. "In developing countries women are challenging customs and governments. They demand health services for their families, education for their daughters. When there are scarce resources, it's women who stretch the food, make a little bit of money last.

"But women from Western Europe and the Americas—parts of Asia too—many of them are quite affluent." She shook her head in mild disgust. "I was thinking of organizing the mothers and aunts and grandmothers from wealthy countries. But since our…our…the-uh episode in Asheville…"

"More like an ambush, it seemed to me. Since then, what?"

"I've become more realistic. Most women refuse to acknowledge the urgency. They've settled into comfortable lives. Earth is in crisis, and they're shopping. I had in mind that you and I could—I thought we could inspire them to turn from their complacency and save Earth for their children."

"And the port-a-potties?"

"How is it that what you most remember about that conversation is port-a-potties? I just mentioned them because you wouldn't quit asking questions. But it's useless, what I was thinking. There's too much greed."

"People's hearts change. You said so yourself."

"Individuals' hearts. This would take a revolution. Millions of people would have to change their priorities. It's not going to happen."

I thought of the many who'd milled around me in Asheville, obviously dismayed. "The supernatural is a sure way to get noticed. You just said that. People would probably pay attention—maybe they'd change if you speak from the clouds or something"

"The western mind—I can't. They'd assume it's some state-of-the-art sound system. Besides, I'm having trouble with the message."

"Try telling the truth."

"The truth? Too much gloom and doom. Americans especially, they want everything to be upbeat. The truth is you're all killing the planet, working toward your own extinction."

I took a bite of cookie, a sip of tea. "You're right, sounds too grim."

She leaned forward, a hint of sparkle returning to her eyes. "Grim but—maybe there is a way to approach this." Reaching for the side handle, she lowered the recliner footrest and stood. "Must have been hunger. Amazing how it can affect one's outlook." With deliberate steps she walked through the kitchen, dropping the afghan over the back of a chair as she passed by.

"Thanks for everything." Without bothering to open the door, she vanished.

"Your shoes!" I called after her.


MY BACK SCREAMED for relief. After hours of working in the garden, of stooping to scatter seeds then covering them with dirt, I was exhausted. I dropped into a lawn chair on the patio. Put my head back. Closed my eyes.

"So I'm thinking we'll start out small." Mary stood before me, again wearing loose trousers and kameez. Her hands were thrust into the windbreaker pockets. Earmuffs protected her ears from the March chill.

She seemed to have regained her energy. "You'll have to organize it, of course, invite a few local women. I'll speak through you, offer some personal comfort the first time. As a hook, that's the term used nowadays, isn't it? Eventually—we'll make it gradual—we'll present the reality that Earth is in a crisis. Then we'll expand, bring in more women, make it a two-day affair so they'll have time to strategize. It will become a movement. You and I, we'll work together to organize a movement."

Me? Organize? Be Mary's voice? That required a woman with self-confidence, an articulate public speaker. Except for starting my business, I had never organized anything. My only experience with confrontation was standing up to the Brothers and Wendell. I'd ended up running away rather than persisting.

But Mary said start out small. I might be able to do that much. Then she would recognize my unsuitability as an organizer, certainly as an adequate mouthpiece.

"I guess I could invite women who come into the store. Invite them all to a—too early for a picnic."

"But you've got the right idea. This works better outside."

"The vernal equinox will soon be here."

"Yes, yes. Very symbolic. Spring, fertility, the beauty of Earth. How about a game? An egg roll maybe?"

"Uh, might be a little juvenile."

"But fun. I want the women to enjoy themselves."

"I thought the idea was to get them to think serious thoughts."

"I'll handle that. So, a week from Saturday?" She adjusted the zipper of her windbreaker. "Gotta run. I'm due in Bosnia."

"Uh, before you go, I'm just curious…"

"Yes?"

"How many languages do you speak? All the places you go, do you…"

"It's the language of the heart that matters. Sometimes I only have to be present." She reached into the pocket of her wind breaker. "I almost forgot this."

A rock. Gray, no bigger than my thumbnail, with dark stripes. "This is from the Aral Sea. A beautiful place. At least it used to be. So many species of fish and mammals. Until humans—"

"Until humans what?"

"They thought it'd do no harm to divert the rivers. Dump chemicals where they pleased. They tested biological weapons on one of the islands. So many children, so many children. This—just a rock, you might say. But without Rock there would be no Earth. It is the foundation of creation." She placed it in the palm of my hand and folded my fingers over it. "Earth is being raped and plundered. Her very survival is at stake. This is to remind you that you have been chosen to work for her restoration." She was gone.

A sensation in the palm of my hand, where Rock nestled, moved up my arm, across my shoulder, coming to rest in the center of my chest. Not like a heart attack, not a tight knot either. More like the creation of a sacred spot from which I felt power radiating.

That evening I crocheted a pouch for Rock, a multi-colored one in threads of red and yellow and blue and green, along with a narrow rope, for it to hang from my neck.

TWELVE WOMEN, MY CIRCLE of friends plus seven who regularly shopped at the store, accepted my invitation to celebrate the vernal equinox. I didn't know what to expect, only that Mary suggested promoting the event as one of food, fun, and the opportunity to honor Earth for the transformation that spring brings. I boiled eggs for the game, prepared a big pot of lentil soup, and baked two loaves of bread. Cloth of Terra covered the kitchen table expanded by four leaves.

In conversation around the table, the women moved comfortably between laughter and seriousness. Once the kitchen had been cleaned—everyone pitching in, as women so often do—we bundled up and went outdoors where the temperature hovered barely over fifty degrees. We rolled hard-boiled eggs down the hill, shrieking in a spirit of competitiveness. As Mary had planned, everyone was having a good time. When we all reached the pond's edge, Marguerite was declared the winner.

My memory of what followed is vague. I've been told that my demeanor changed. The women whispered among themselves as my face took on a vacant expression, my skin turning pale, my gaze staring ahead. They quieted as I walked among them then stopped beneath the willow tree. I closed my eyes.

I lifted my hands high, they told me. A bright light appeared above my head. The women moved closer, extending their arms toward the sky too. Everything became quiet: birds, insects, even the wind. What first appeared as a whirl of mist began to coalesce until it had taken the shape of a woman. A vaporous specter, she wore baggy pants and kameez, and stood beside me but without her feet touching the ground. A woman's voice, resonant yet gentle, came from my mouth, utterances in English with a Middle-Eastern accent.

Strangely, every woman heard a different message. According to one, the voice told her that her husband, unemployed, would soon find work. Another woman was assured her rebellious daughter would turn from her ways.

"Who are you?" they all asked in unison as the light began to ascend.

"I am Mary, Mother of Yeshu." The gossamer form faded then vanished.

I opened my eyes and looked around. Dazed. I remembered standing by the pond, lifting my arms. After that—it was like I stood on the edge of a canyon wall, my body ready to dive over the edge into a vast chasm of nothingness. I had jumped. But instead of dropping to the canyon floor, I floated over the garden, over the fields, over the mountains, my essence outside my body. I had become Mary. Or had Mary become me? Words had come from my mouth, I was told, but they hadn't been my words. The voice not my voice.

Once I came to, I felt exhausted, as if I had run a marathon or filled a barn full of hay. Exhausted enough, confused enough, that I didn't want to do it—whatever *it* was—ever again.

I expected the nearby towns to be abuzz with news that something strange had happened at Willow Pond Farm. That I was mentally unstable. Not even a murmur. Each woman who had attended came into the store, though, bought an item or more, smiled as I bagged it or handed over change, then clasped my hand and whispered, "Thank you."

Amelia, with no further explanation, expressed gratitude for the healing power she'd experienced.

JEZEBEL LAY ON THE PATIO BRICK warmed by the day's sun, her nose turned into the gentle evening breeze. I sat in a lawn chair drinking a cup of hot tea brewed with mint from my herb garden. After a busier day than usual, the store was closed, receipts totaled. I'd be glad when apprentices arrived for the summer. There were yet tomatoes, cucumbers, and squash to plant. The previous year more customers than ever, several restaurants among them, had driven out to buy fresh vegetables.

Jezebel rose, whimpered, and began pacing the width of the patio.

"We need to plan a second gathering." Mary leaned against the nearby maple tree. She wore a hijab, and a tunic over pants. Like a seasoned farmer, she moved a stem of dried grass from one side of her mouth to the other.

"Please, no," I moaned. "I didn't like—you know, it really was not a pleasant experience. It was like being in a coma."

"Don't go comparing it to a coma," she scolded. "Poor Rudolpho. Fell from the scaffolding while building the cathedral—now when would that have been? 1630? Forty? You were saying?"

"It was exhausting, whatever happened, even without all the preparations. You need to find yourself a twenty-year-old."

"Humph! Who's going to pay attention to a twenty-year-old inviting them to one of our sessions?"

She stepped over to the low brick wall bordering the patio. Perched herself atop the ledge, propped her knees up, and rested her elbows on her knees. Quite different from the lethargic, discouraged Mary who'd recently lain back in my recliner and announced her retirement.

"Is that what you call them, sessions? Makes it sound like you're a therapist."

"What term would you use?"

"Séance? I'm kidding."

"Apparitions, the church calls them. Let's avoid the church's term for anything."

"Appearances. I've heard that word used. Like in Lourdes. And Vietnam."

Her buoyant attitude from minutes earlier gave way to slouched shoulders. Her eyes became moist. "Ah, Vietnam. If it's not persecution, it's war. So many suffered. So many. They've needed me there." She wiped the tears with her sleeve. "Those European missionaries made me look like something from Raphael. What Asian is going to believe that a woman who looks like the colonizer cares about their wellbeing?"

She spit the strand of long grass out of her mouth. "We need to do it again, another—okay, I'll accept *appearance*. Two weeks. Is that enough time to get ready?"

"I told you I'm tired. It's spring. There's a lot of work to do around here. Besides, you said your purpose is that, that—Project: Earth Rescue, you called it. But when they told me what you said, it had nothing to do with the Earth. More like Dear Abby."

"If they think something will be expected of them, they won't come back."

"Why me? I've hardly seen you since I was a kid. Then when I first moved here, you popped in…over…up…down…I don't know where from. I appreciated that, I really did. I was discouraged. Now all these years later you're back with big plans." I couldn't help myself. I started to cry. "I want to know, why me?"

She rose from the brick wall and came to stand in front of me. Her playful, almost flippant, attitude of earlier minutes suddenly turned serious. I became aware of qualities artists have recognized all these centuries. Radiance combined with a deep sorrow. Her eyes and her posture declared *I'll stand beside you; I will not allow you to be defeated.*

"You were a special girl," she said, "with a strong drive to understand. What your father considered irreverent, I admired. During those years when you pushed me away, I kept watch. Not all of your decisions were wise ones. You know that now.

Later you had the courage to stand up to the Brothers. Over time—it never comes quickly—you've become a wise woman. I sense that behind your current reluctance is a strength that will serve our cause well."

A wise woman, *our* cause. Like we were a team.

"But if you really want me to go find somebody else," she said, "if you don't want to..."

"No, no, I'll try it one more time. It's just that—it's so much work. Can we not include food this time?"

"Like Yeshu used to say, 'If you're going to change people's hearts, you've got to feed them.' By the way, only a woman would have been able to feed all those people with just five loaves and two fish. Prepare what you did the last time. I'll stretch it. I liked the mint tea. Can you do that again?"

"Can I! The mint's taken over."

"We'll work out the menu details later. I just want you to start thinking about it. And inviting the women. We've got a lot of work to do, the two of us." She looked toward the west. "Oh-oh, sun's going down. It's so comfortable here I get to relaxing and almost—" She was gone.

I stood there, fingering Rock inside its pouch hanging from my neck.

*Asheville Citizen-Times*
Virgin Mary makes local appearance

August 8—On Saturday mornings for the past two and a half months, many witnesses claim to have seen the Virgin Mary at Willow Pond Farm, near Kona. They describe the apparitions as summoned by health-food store owner Elizabeth McNair going into a trance. The Virgin Mary's voice comes from McNair's mouth.

Valerie Codgetal, who has attended several appearances, told reporters, "You can't see her clearly. She's sort of fuzzy. She looks like an Indian, the kind from India, with dark skin and black and gray hair tied in a knot on top of her head. She wears loose trousers and an Indian-looking top." McNair declines interviews and does not allow news cameras on site.

Sources say Saturday was the Virgin Mary's tenth visitation at Willow Pond Farm and the largest to date, with over 70 women in attendance. According to Codgetal, "We come on Friday evening and spend the night there so that we're present when Mary appears Saturday morning. Fridays offer a chance to be with other women and develop strategies for saving the environment. That's why Mary comes, you know, to talk about how bad the environmental situation is and to inspire us to save the planet."

To accommodate such a gathering McNair supplies tents for overnight stays and temporary toilets. Meals are potluck, supplemented by soup and homemade bread, baked, some claim, by the Virgin Mary herself.

According to Lois Markowsky, who is spending the summer learning about organic gardening at McNair's farm, "Mother Mary says the land belongs to all generations, those who came before us and those who will come after. Humanity's survival depends on honoring the communities of all who inhabit Earth, plants and animals."

Homemaker Clorissa Weaver, who has attended two visitations, told reporters, "The Blessed Mother reminds us that we can't trust elected officials to keep the air breathable, the water drinkable. We all must act in defense of our families and communities."

In an interview by phone Archbishop Luis Bolin stated, "This is clearly a commercial gimmick, a shrewd businesswoman making a fortune off of women's gullibility. It's important that we get word out that this is not a legitimate religious experience."

Rev. Edmund Anderson, of Bethel Baptist Church, also expressed concern: "Women, we know, are highly susceptible to the power of suggestion. Ever since Eve they've been prone to falling victim to deception."

~~~

FRIDAY MORNINGS MARY arrived carrying her leather satchel, its contents a mystery, as she always wore the same garments during the appearances: loose trousers and kameez. Right away the two of us began to make bread, proofing the yeast, buttering the pans. Working in harmony, we folded, pressed, rolled, until the desired elasticity was achieved. The bread's quality depended on the bakers' frame of mind, Mary always mentioned as the yeasty fragrance filled the house.

For a while our conversation focused on the next morning's appearance. "You need to know what I'll say," she told me. "There will likely be questions later." At other times we both were absorbed in our own thoughts.

Some time after five p.m. the crunching sound of gravel in the long driveway and Jezebel's barking interrupted the mountain quiet. In groups of two or three the first few months, then by carloads, then by buses from as far away as Atlanta and Washington, women brought sleeping bags and suitcases or backpacks. The clang of hammers echoed through the valley as they drove tent stakes into the ground. During these evening hours my circle of local friends served as greeters, assisting where needed, offering a welcoming beverage and homemade cookies.

As soon as women began to arrive Mary went upstairs. Come sundown, I joined her in the guest room to mark the beginning of Jewish Shabbat. For me it was a poignant ritual, our placing two lit candles on a table, covering our eyes as she prayed. Afterwards, while I went out to meet guests, she stayed upstairs, not to be seen until nine o'clock the next morning. Except by me. Later in the evening, when everyone seemed settled, I joined her for a competitive game of Scrabble.

THE WARMTH OF THE MORNING sun was starting to erase the mist hanging over the valley. Heavy shadows lingered. In the distance could be heard the crowing of roosters, the low of cows. On the slope leading down to the pond, women, some youthful and slender, others older and of more substantial build, spread out in a semi-circle. Most of the older women had brought along lawn chairs. Younger ones sat on blankets, resting elbows on
~~~

their knees or sitting in a half-lotus position. Eyes turned on me, all waited in silent anticipation.

I stood under the willow tree wearing a long white dress. From my neck hung the multi-colored pouch I'd crocheted for Rock. Eyes closed, I clasped it firmly. My eyes glazed over, I let go of Rock. I lifted my arms and mumbled, calling forth Mary. At that point I lost awareness and have only vague recollections. Most of what I know came from her pre-appearance summary, supplemented by those who attended.

Soon she stood beside me in gossamer form, her feet not touching the ground. Though my mouth moved, it was not my voice.

"My daughters, she who has ears to hear, let her hear." A pause. "Let your body, your thoughts, become one with Earth…. Hear as Earth hears, for her survival and yours depend on heeding the signs….

"…Listen now to Soil. For millennia, she was nourished by death and decay, holding in tenderness spirits that were absorbed into her. Because of them she was able, according to her own timetable, to offer gifts of berry and grain. Now humans have replaced her natural fertility with nitrogen and phosphorus, boron and chlorine." There was a pause. "Soil is fragile and must be cared for.

"…Listen to Hill…. She wraps herself around this valley, offering protection from Wind, when it is in an icy mood. Once Hill's jagged peaks reached higher into the heavens. Water and Wind swept across her, carrying away Soil, leaving hill rounded, like a young woman with child. In other places she is more like a woman of years, marked by cracks and crevices. Native people left trails across her and honored her gifts. Now those intent upon monetary gain strip her pinnacles, pry her open, and consume her viscera."

Until this point most women attending for the first time were mainly curious, staring first at the translucent image then at me. Some extended their hands as if from a distance they might touch Mary. After a few minutes, though, the need to confirm the corporeality of what they saw and heard seemed to dissolve. One by one they closed their eyes.

"…Listen to Tree….Her roots stretch down, down. My, what she has seen in her time. She was once a mere seed, a babe that needed special care. Water, nutrients provided by Soil. During periods of draught Tree sent roots deeper in search of Water. An arm died, but she sent out a new one. Sometimes Tree sacrificed branches to be used for fires that provided warmth for humans. Now she struggles against disease caused by acid rain, the heating of the planet.

"…Listen to Water…. She springs from a secret place in Hill's crevasses, forming rivulets that join to become mighty rivers. Eventually Water makes her way to pond and sea. For generations she has quenched thirst, nurtured crops, been home to fish and crab and salamander. She once was pure, but industries released their chemicals into streams and lakes. Fertilizers and pesticides have been washed into waterways.

"Women, the future of Earth depends on you. Now is not the time to passively wait for others to rescue her. You must take charge with boldness and courage. You have the intelligence to help others understand the crisis. You have the skills of leadership. Even if no one has allowed you the opportunity to use them, you will discover your ability to inspire others to share in the sacrifice to save Creation.

"Hold Earth as you would a lover on the verge of dying. Close to your heart. Love her unselfishly, as she has loved you. Give your life for her if that is required."

As Mary's image faded, I emerged from the trance feeling groggy, as if waking from a deep sleep.

Throughout the summer and autumn, Mary's weekly appearances ran a similar course. (In the winter she headquartered in southern Europe, her intention there also to inspire women to rescue Earth.) After each appearance one or two women—accustomed, it seemed, to harried lives and the bombardment of sounds—would peer around anxiously, waiting for something more to happen. Most, though, with eyes closed, sat back in their lawn chairs or kept a meditative posture on their blankets. They remained quiet for half an hour, sometimes longer. After a while a faint moan would rise, increasing in volume as more joined, until a keen echoed against the hills.

Gradually women stood. Some, carrying their chairs or folded blankets, whispered a word of thanks to me and returned to cars or buses to journey home. Others stayed for a lunch of bread Mary and I had baked, along with food each had brought to share, spread out on a long table covered with Cloth of Terra.

THE DIFFIDENCE RESULTING from my childhood began to give way to a sense of competence and self-assurance. Being at the forefront of Mary's movement, I no longer felt peripheral to a community but central to it.

I became reconciled to myself, honoring the little girl who had dared question the teachings of the church. Growing to love the over-weight Elizabeth, the not-so-hefty one; the one who had tried to be a perfectionist and the one who failed; the woman who was a good parent and the one who abandoned her family.

In college I either slept or daydreamed through compulsory world history classes. Now, kneading dough on floured boards or drinking tea with Mary, I was privy to private lessons spanning centuries. Not lectures centered around wars, their causes, their battles, their generals, their aftermaths, but Mary's stories about accompanying women of Africa, Europe, Asia, and the Americas. Women who taught their children not to block the path of a soldier or look a white man in the eye, not to get caught up in a crowd throwing stones. Women who risked their own lives walking dangerous roadways to get their children to safety, bending their bodies in arid fields to grow food for their families. Women striving to get an education.

On Sundays, with Mary and the crowds gone, I recovered in the rocking chair by the meditation table in my bedroom. Rocking, thinking. Sometimes about history. How it isn't just the past but also what's ahead, a progression, each era building on the next, each generation wanting for its children a life of peace and freedom. For many this has meant freedom from back-breaking toil. But inventions intended to improve life end up in landfills. Mercury and lead from dumps seep into streams and gradually make their way into drinking water.

How do you stop the course of a history on the verge of destroying the planet? I wondered. Through drastic action, Mary urged. Not action supported by the powerful, whose investments and financial wealth depend on degrading the earth. No, I was convinced Mary was right: If Earth was going to survive, women would have to do it.

# Chapter 15

"I NEED TO TALK," Nada Sue said.

It was during the second summer of Mary's appearances, on a Wednesday afternoon.. Without any makeup on Nada Sue had lost her prom queen look. Dark rings circled her eyes.

Elbows propped on my kitchen table, head resting in the palms of her hands, she stared down at the table. "I'm sorry," she mumbled. "I know it's all about protecting the environment, and that's important, but I just can't come to any more of these, these…The Virgin Mary. The Holy Mother. Mother Mary. Whatever she's called." She removed her elbows, let her bright red fingernails trace the grain of the oak. "I've got too many issues."

"Issues?"

Nada Sue's eyes met mine. Her voice strengthened. "You know, I lost my beloved Paul—it's been almost twenty-five years ago. Watching him die—the whole experience left me—well, it was a lot more than him dying."

She reached into a pocket for a tissue. A few seconds passed while she wiped tears from her eyes and blew her nose.

"What I haven't talked about is that at the same time he was diagnosed I found out I was pregnant. Our three kids were already teenagers, and with his diagnosis it looked like I'd have to finish raising them on my own. Besides, while Paul was alive, I knew I'd have to devote my energy to caring for him. We decided—it wasn't an easy decision—but we decided—I got an abortion. Well, I made the mistake of telling my mother, who told my father, who told our minister, who convinced them I was going to hell."

Nada Sue paused to take a deep breath. I reached over to grasp her hand.

"Can you imagine what it was like for me? Cut off from my parents and the church at the most difficult time in my life?"

She pulled her hand from beneath mine and pounded the table with her fist. "I want nothing to do with religion."

"B-but, I'm sure Mary doesn't have any tolerance for that kind of rejection. And religion—our movement has nothing to do with a church."

"I guess I'm the one who has no tolerance. No tolerance for anything that reminds me of those horrible years. When I moved here, that's when I became acquainted with Wiccan. I get the spiritual benefits without all the shit."

ANOTHER CONVERSATION in the kitchen. This time Peaches, the most highly educated of my circle of friends, sat opposite me at the kitchen table.

"Yes, I've seen it with my own eyes, that mirage down there. I'm not accusing you of manipulating anyone or anything. It's just that—it's just that I'm a doubter by nature. I'm sorry, but I can't take part in this hocus-pocus."

As a result of Nada Sue's and Peaches' decisions, Marguerite decided not to participate either. Amelia and Fran continued to attend the appearances. Amelia, it seemed, because she sought healing related to something in her past she couldn't speak of. Fran, because she was already an activist committed to the environment.

In spite of these departures, Mary's plan was taking hold, albeit on a lesser scale than she intended. Women returned to their communities, eager to do what they could to rescue Earth. They recycled, carried groceries home in canvas bags, hung laundry on clothes lines. They urged their children to turn off lights when leaving a room. They organized friends to write letters to their representatives—though in private Mary confided her skepticism about getting politicians to support any effort not in their immediate interest. Four women from Kentucky organized their neighbors to spend Saturdays gathering debris in the Upper Cumberland River Basin. A woman from Kingsport began to write regular newspaper columns about protecting the environment—before she switched to humorous musings on local events. A woman from a beach town in South Carolina got her community involved in protecting the eggs of sea turtles during summer months.

But it became evident that instead of persevering, women would start a project, get involved for four or five months, then lose interest. No one expressed a willingness to challenge the government, large corporations, or powerful people who benefited from exploiting Earth. No one was willing to move beyond simple projects and risk status, relationships, or livelihood on behalf of the planet.

Then several white women, having attended multiple times, started treating the gatherings like a reunion. Friday nights, seated apart from the others—on logs, lawn chairs, and blankets—they didn't discuss how they might rescue Earth. Instead they carried on lively conversations about their children, celebrities, and whether the world would end in 2018, as a popular magazine claimed Nostradamus had predicted.

In spite of my efforts, few of the white women reached out to African-American women who came. Apparently word got around the black community that even though Mary—herself of dark complexion—had an inspiring message, it was an unwelcoming crowd for women of color.

Mary had planned to bring women together—black, brown and white—appeal to their hearts, so that as daughters, wives, mothers, and grandmothers they would pledge to rescue the planet from destruction. She'd hoped that around homemade bread served on a table covered with Cloth of Terra, they would become a sisterhood of activists who claimed their power to alter the course of history. They would pressure legislators, neighbors, their partners. Teach their children to consume less and use fewer fossil fuels. Finally, like other women Mary had accompanied over the centuries, they would confront those with power, even put their lives on the line if that was required.

"LISTEN TO THE BIRDS calling out to their young," Mary said through my mouth. A moment of silence allowed the birds to speak for themselves. The *per-tee, per-tee* of the cardinal, the *drink your tea, drink your tea* of the towhee.

"And beneath you—listen to moles, to insects, burrowing under the soil." Many in attendance strained to hear a variety of creatures scratching near the surface of the earth.

"Feel the breeze," she said, inviting each woman to relax her body, let her face and bare arms become conscious of the gentle wind passing over her. "That's memory's breath. The breeze remembers the day you were born. It remembers when this was virgin forest, when ancient elms and spruce spread out their branches to greet each day."

The scent of a recently plowed field drifted over them.

"You are one with Earth and with other women who inhabit it. Women protect and conserve. They gather water in desert climates, knowing the preciousness of each drop that falls from the gourd or the bucket. Women linger to study every plant, to understand its value in healing and nurturing. For millennia women have sought to use resources for the well being of the whole clan—not just the strong and able-bodied.

"Release your struggles to be included in men's structures of power while you still remember in your very DNA the skills of your foremothers. Skills that will enable Earth and future generations to survive."

A NEW GROUP HAD FORMED. Friday evenings, in the area where the light of the fire merged with the surrounding darkness, they sat in a circle. They beat drums decorated with intricate carvings, some shaped like an hourglass, some like a bowl, some shallow in depth, some deep. A common rhythm emerged. Different pitches of boom, thump, and tap echoed across the valley.

"I have nothing against drumming," Mary told me on a Friday morning. While the yeasty aroma of baking bread wafted through the house, we stood at the sink washing and drying bowls and utensils. "In the right context. In fact I appreciate drums in the hands of native peoples seeking unity with Earth's rhythms, with the heartbeat of Creator. And drums can be therapeutic, I've heard. Those women, the ones who've been bringing theirs, they're searching for inner peace. But our cause is not about inner peace. It's about becoming agitated enough to take action."

Also, on successive Friday evenings a local entrepreneur, Betsy Padgett, erected a canopy over a folding table. She spread out the contents of two large suitcases: oils and compounds for aroma therapy, Native American dream catchers. She branded herself a Crystal Resonance Therapist, advising women about how to select a crystal based on their zodiac sign or the feel of the gem. While some sat around the campfire beating their drums and a few others talked of how to save Earth, Betsy read tarot cards—for a small fee, of course.

"You've got to speak with her," Mary told me. With a flour-covered hand she brushed a strand of hair from her face. "She's distorting my whole reason for bringing women together. I want them to take action."

"What do I tell her?"

"What I just said. You can blame me."

"But she's sincere. Sure, she makes a little money, but the women like getting their—"

"Her sincerity is the problem. The women are getting off track, and—well, she's diluting my message."

A few minutes later I was on the phone with Betsy.

"But I *am* supporting the mission. Crystals are a product of Earth too."

"Urgency," I said.

"What do you mean?"

"She's talking about urgency. That we have to do something to save plants and animals, humans too, from extinction. Immediately."

"That's exactly what I'm promoting. Action. Crystals speak. The cards speak."

"No, you're getting the women to focus on themselves, to think about their own future, their own healing, rather than Earth's healing. Please keep coming. Your kindness and sensitivity, the way you—you're really important to these gatherings. But if you come, she wants you to leave your inventory at home."

"All right, but I think it's wrong. We need intercessory objects to help us develop a renewed love for the earth."

"She is the intercessory. The intercessory between women and Earth."

From then on Betsy came without her merchandise, and while several women honored Mary's request to no longer bring their drums, others decided to stay home. Amelia and Fran denounced the undemocratic nature of the appearances and quit coming.

DURING THE EARLY SUMMER between Angelica's first and second year at Duke, she sometimes took a break from her studies and drove to the farm on appearance weekends. Occasionally she stayed overnight. At other times she headed back to her apartment after dark. She kept bathrooms stocked with toilet paper, returned dishes to the cupboards after they'd been washed, distributed literature about protecting the planet.

During appearances she sat on the ground near the top of the hill, arms wrapped around her knees, and listened to Mary speak through my mouth: "It rains when it shouldn't. It's dry where it's always been wet. Just because you don't realize you're breathing polluted air doesn't mean it isn't polluted. And do not assume that just because you have not seen the rubber trees of Borneo, the margay, or the Arabian gazelle, that they have nothing to do with you. She is a web of all creation, Earth is. Cut one strand, and the web is weakened. Several strands and it falls apart."

By her third trip back home, Angelica's smiles had become more strained, the worry lines across her forehead more prominent. In my flurry of activity I noticed but failed to take the time to acknowledge her unrest.

"MOM, I NEED TO TALK."

I was rushing in the direction of the newly constructed bathhouse, a plunger in hand. "Catch me in a few minutes."

Once that problem was handled, women from Atlanta were shrieking. I picked up the offending black snake with a heavy stick, carried it over to the other side of the house, and threw it into the weeds.

"Mom, please, I can't stay. I came to talk with you. It'll only take a few minutes."

"Ouch, ouch," a woman hollered as she ran toward us. She'd burned her hand while lighting a lantern. "Run in and break off a piece of the aloe plant," I told Angelica.

The burn taken care of, Angelica was trying to keep up with my hurried strides toward the house. I stopped abruptly, grasped her shoulders. "I'm sorry," I said and gave her an energetic hug. "Now what is it you want to talk with me about?"

"Not here. Can't we find some place that's private? Down by the pond?"

A floodlight on a utility pole cast a long narrow swath of light down the slope. At the edge of the pond, shadows nearly hid a cluster of women engaged in earnest conversation. Angelica tugged on the sleeve of my t-shirt and pulled me over to an area that was darker still.

"Now then, what is it?" I asked, trying to mask my impatience.

"I'm going to quit school."

"What? You can't. It's your dream." I turned to climb back up the hill. In my mind the conversation was over.

"Excuse us." From the shadows a woman in the cluster called after me. I approached them, at the same time turning the disapproving pucker of my lips into a friendly smile. "We're all curious, when did you first encounter the Virgin Mary?"

"She prefers being referred to as the Blessed Mother or Mother Mary or just plain Mary. I was a girl of about nine." The story followed, of being exiled to my room and how Mary appeared in a corner of the ceiling, sometimes up in the grapefruit tree.

"I'm sorry," Angelica interrupted, "but I need to speak with my mother for a few minutes. It's personal." She took me by the hand. The women muttered an apology and turned to walk uphill toward the tents.

"Like I said, I want to quit school. When Mary says to listen, I close my eyes and—and what I hear—I hear insecticide spray hissing as it escapes a canister. I hear explosives tear away the top of a mountain, the trees groaning as they tumble into the valley."

She drew the sleeve of her blouse to her face to wipe away tears. "Earth—I hear her cry, Mom. I hear Earth cry."

I pulled Angelica to my bosom and stroked her hair. "I know you do," I whispered. "I know you do. And it's one of the things I love about you, your sensitivity to nature. But it's also why you're in school. And why you can't quit your program."

She stepped back. "You don't understand how academia works. The constant pressure to publish, get the right credentials so you can—I know I don't have any political or economic power, but I do have the power of my convictions. And my convictions tell me I've got to put my body on the line."

"Your body? Nonsense. Besides, I've invested too much money in your education to let it all go to waste." I turned abruptly and began to take large, deliberate steps uphill. Angelica walked behind, but instead of following me into the house, she got in her car and headed back to Durham.

A TUESDAY EVENING, the kind of summer evening that inspires insects to sing energetic songs. Trash and clutter from the weekend were cleaned up by this time of the week. The store had closed for the day. The two college students devoting their summer to learning about organic gardening were putting tools away. Soon they would retire to the cabin.

I lay stretched out on the chaise lounge on the patio, the evening breeze cooling my skin. I was just drifting off to sleep when—

"Elizabeth."

I opened my eyes. "What are you doing here?"

Mary stood beside me, face turned toward the pond. "There's something I want to show you."

At the pond's edge, without any concern of getting wet, she stepped in the water and reached into a cluster of cattails. "Look at this." In her hand she held a frog, its haunches of mottled gray, its face a bright green.

I gasped. An extra leg grew out of its cream-colored belly. "Poor little one," Mary said, stroking the frog's back. "Here, hold it." I drew away. "Come now. It's as important to God's creation as you are." I tentatively extended my hand.

Neither of us spoke for a while. Against my will, I started to cry, tears dropping onto the animal frozen in fear in the palm of my hand.

Mary's voice was gentle. "Why are you crying?"

"I guess because I'm afraid."

"Of what?"

"Not afraid of…afraid for. Afraid for what this means. That creation is out of whack."

"My appearances—it's obvious nothing's going to come of it all. That's why *you* must do something."

And she was gone. Leaving me to stand by the edge of the pond, a mutant frog in hand. In my dreams that night I held orange salamanders with one eye, gray lizards with two tails, toads with no legs at all.

Early the following morning, wearing jeans and a t-shirt, I went outside. Patches of glistening moisture dotted the landscape. I walked down to the pond and stretched out on the wet grass, lying there a long time, eyes closed. Birds sang, clearly thrilled by the dawn. Insects whirred a sigh of contentment. A warm tongue licked my face; Jezebel too was rejoicing in the day.

Standing up, arms lifted, I began to sing a melody without words, celebratory in tone. But before long the song had turned into a dirge and I was crying.

Dear Mom,

I planned to come by the farm again and try to get your blessing now that you've had time to think about it, but things moved more quickly than expected. I hope you'll understand.

I quit my studies.

It's not the program. I love every minute I spend in the classroom and out in the field. I'm quitting because my teachers testify in Washington and consult with groups about global warming and the harm we're doing to the planet, but their scientific expertise is ignored. So what good is it if I get a degree but can't get past the public's apathy?

A chance to join a group of activists has come up suddenly, and I'm going to take it. I'm not free to tell you exactly what we'll be doing, only that our goal is to bring the crisis to the public's attention and make the exploitation of Earth less profitable for business.

Our cell has to operate in secrecy, so communication will be difficult. The larger organization has computer geeks on board, though, who are able to create programs that make it hard to trace us. So even if you don't hear from me, I hope you'll try to stay in touch. I'll try too, but I can't promise anything. Send messages to w183@torbox3.onion.

Mom, you've had high hopes for me getting my degree, but you more than anyone know how much I love Earth, its people, its animals, its plants. To live a life of integrity I must do everything I can to protect it all. I want to make a difference.

I love you.

Angelica


EVERYTHING HAPPENED IN rapid succession: the mutant frog, Angelica's letter. Now this.

It was early on a Saturday morning. Too early for Mary to be descending the stairs. Though there she was, carrying her leather satchel.

I stopped measuring coffee into the basket of a commercial urn. "What's going on?"

"Come on, let's get this over with." She set the satchel down by the door leading to the kitchen stoop.

Anyone getting up late that morning missed it. The visitation started shortly after seven, instead of the usual nine-o'clock hour.

"Don't expect your children to clean up the mess you've made of Earth. The day will come when the cause that should have been your own becomes the passion of your child. Believe me, it is better to have died yourself than to watch the life drained from your beloved son or daughter."

And she was gone.

"I drove all this way for something that lasted less than a minute?" women complained.

Vigorously shaking my head to escape the fog of the trance, I stumbled back to the house as fast as I could.

I barely made it in time to see Mary pick up her satchel. "Ciao," was all she said, the word's significance obvious. The project at the farm was finished.

Without being told, the women sensed it too. When they'd quit grumbling about the brevity of the appearance, they quietly carried their sleeping bags and suitcases to their cars and buses. A few stayed behind to tear down the tents and clean the bathhouse.

As soon as everyone had left, I grabbed Cloth of Terra from the long table on the patio, wadded its great length into my arms, and ran upstairs. I threw myself across the bed and sobbed into the folds of the multi-colored fabric. The rest of the day and through the night I lay there, getting up only to go to the bathroom.

The following morning, trailed by Jezebel, I hiked the perimeter of the property, hands thrust in the pockets of my jeans, boots stomping through the weeds. *After all I put into making this a gathering place, meeting her specifications. So the project doesn't move along as fast as she wants it to. What did she expect, a miracle or something?*

An old emotion returned, one going all the way back to childhood: the feeling of not belonging. Yes, I still had my farm and store, but Mary had made it something bigger, part of a plan to rescue the planet. And I was central to its success.

"What about me?" I yelled to the hills, to the pond, to the fields. "What about me?"

I NEEDED TO FIND MARY. I needed to convince her to return to my North Carolina farm and resume the visitations. If she wouldn't return, she could at least give me a few words of guidance. Guidance about how a sixty-seven-year-old woman can make the rest of her life count for something. But how would I find one who doesn't operate according to the logic of the living?

The Scrabble box. Friday evenings, just the two of us played Scrabble upstairs, though keeping her languages straight always presented a challenge for Mary. Now I set the box on the round kitchen table. I turned the wooden tiles upside down in the lid, shuffled them around. Closed my eyes and drew one. An R. Raleigh? Rocky Mountains? Rhode Island?

A capricious decision, yes. But there had been the *ciao* farewell. And don't all roads lead to Rome?

# A Vision

*He leadeth me in the paths of righteousness for his namesake. He leadeth me… Aunt Rachel, prepare a place for me to lie in comfort. My bones ache from nights spent upon this filthy prison mattress. Wave a fan across my shoulders, Aunt Rachel, bring relief from this awful heat. Fill a tub of warm water, so that I may bathe. Even when she could go free, Aunt Rachel chose to stay with me. No one can claim that I failed to follow Holy Scripture: "Masters, give unto your servants that which is just and equal; knowing that ye also have a Master in heaven." In Africa the darkies were but naked heathens. With the war's end, they have returned to their pagan ways, killing their masters, fighting each other over scraps of food. Yankees do not understand how much better they lived under our care. Listen, Elizabeth, what I did was in God's name, to thwart Yankee aggression against his beloved South. Along with Wilkes, I was but "an instrument in the hands of the Almighty to punish this proud and licentious people." * [2] He leadeth me in the paths of righteousness for…*

---

[2]from the affidavit of Louis Weichmann, compiled by Benn Pittman in The Assassination of President Lincoln and the Trial of Conspirators (New York: Moore, Walstach and Baldwin, Publishers, 1865).

# Chapter 16



KELETAL REMAINS OF THE COLISSEUM loom against the brilliant blue sky. Elizabeth is still unsettled from her encounter with a burly young man clad in the tunic and armor of a Roman soldier. Everyone around stopped to stare as he gave her the finger and let loose a string of profanity. In English.

It has to be a demeaning job, she decides, feeding his family by wearing a ridiculous costume, wheedling money from tourists. Is it her fault he made an error in judgment by standing beside her and having a cohort take a Polaroid picture? Elizabeth's purpose—except for these few forays to ancient sites—is to find Mary, not amass photos of herself at tourist attractions.

Across the street she feels safe, but her heart's still pounding rapidly. She takes several deep breaths before opening her map. Santa Maria in Aracoeli isn't far away. A stop there, then back to the convent to rest awhile. She's walked a lot today.

Eyes fixed on the map, without pausing to look up, she takes a step in the direction of the church. Something blocks her way. She stumbles and trips forward, instinctively reaching out to catch her fall. Instead of palms slapping against pavement, as she expects, she's grasping the arm of a wheelchair.

"Signora." A little girl extends a small ceramic bowl and shakes it to make the coins inside rattle. Standing up straight now, Elizabeth drops her gaze from the bowl to the child's torso. To grimy pants folded under the stubs of legs. To thin arms poking out of capped sleeves. Up to olive-toned cheeks smudged with dirt, to her mouth, curved upward, smiling at this potential donor. Elizabeth stares into the little girl's eyes. And gasps.

Mary's eyes. Their gazes lock.

Without looking away Elizabeth wriggles out of the backpack on her shoulders. She unzips the side compartment and takes out her wallet, all the while wondering how much money Mary expects. One euro? Surely no more than ten. There's a commotion behind her. Instinctively she turns. Her reflexes are too slow. In that brief moment when her attention is averted, her wallet is grabbed from her hands. Helplessly she watches as a teenage girl runs off, pushing the girl in the wheelchair in front of her.

"Thief," Elizabeth yells after them. "Help, police."

Soon a crowd has gathered, making tsk-tsk sounds and expressing sympathy for her plight.

"You've got to watch out for those damn gypsies," an Italian man says in English.

"They'll divert your attention then steal the shirt off your back," a woman with a British accent says.

Opening a travel book, an American woman points to a paragraph. "See, Rick Steves warns about them. Right here. They look for tourists."

As a man in uniform approaches, the crowd drifts away. He's a good looking young officer, with short cropped hair that accentuates his chiseled cheekbones, a smile that surely has made the hearts of women flutter. But looks and charm go only so far, and it soon becomes apparent that theft is too common an occurrence for him to get all worked up over this situation. He takes her name and the address of the convent where she's staying and says she'll be contacted if her wallet shows up. Which isn't likely, he adds.

Fortunately she carries her passport and credit cards in a money belt. Right now a calming glass of wine seems more inviting than the dark interior of another church. She heads north from the Colosseum in search of an ATM.

AT A TABLE FOR FOUR, under a striped awning, she stares at her wine glass. She was targeted. A sixty-seven-year-old woman, unaccustomed to foreign travel. Alone. First the fake Roman soldier cursing at her, then being accosted by gypsies—the little girl having Mary's eyes—that was what persuaded Elizabeth to take out her wallet. *A foolish woman. I am a very foolish woman.*

Out of habit she brings her hand to her neck, reaching for Rock, a comfort at moments like this. The sole fact of its having endured the harshness of weather and time has more than once reminded her that her problems are fleeting.

It's gone!

She shoves her hand inside her blouse to see if it fell there, runs fingers along the edge of her bra. She pushes the chair back, jarring the table. Red wine splatters onto the white linen tablecloth. She crawls around, her hands search the cement floor. There's no sign of Rock or of its crocheted pouch.

Maybe she forgot to put it back on after showering this morning. Being away from home, awakening so early, her schedule's still out of sync, her routine disrupted. Paying the bill, she leaves the glass of partially drunk wine and rushes to the subway station.

Instead of waiting for the convent's wobbly elevator, she climbs the stairs as quickly as she's able. Her key gets jammed in the lock. "Come on, come on," she coaxes. Finally, after convincing herself to calm down, she gives the key a gentle turn. The door opens.

She searches under the bed, in the bathroom, among her clothes. Skirt, tops, and pants hang on a metal rack in the corner; her underwear's in one of two narrow dresser drawers, toiletries in the other. Her hands glide across every surface, shake out each item of clothing.

Stretched out on the bed, crucifix hanging on the wall above her head, fingers clasped across her chest, she tries to understand what happened. Slowly it comes to her. The little girl in the wheelchair. While her companion grabbed the wallet, the little girl—how could she have possibly—?

"Mary," Elizabeth says aloud. "She set me up. She took Rock."

It was an attempt to be generous, give a poor girl a few Euros. So why would Mary interfere? Maybe she was trying to communicate something. But why wouldn't she just appear and explain herself, as she's done before?

Elizabeth closes her eyes. In her mind she sees the little girl. Not as she was only an hour earlier but clean, hair combed. And she has legs. A healthy girl, a happy girl. She's running after something, laughing as she reaches toward it: the multi-colored pouch that holds Rock.

AT BREAKFAST THE NEXT MORNING Elizabeth still feels unsettled. She sits at the table nearest the entrance to the breakfast area, only a few feet from the alabaster statuette of Mary with a halo of lights, and next to a screenless window looking out over the Edenesque courtyard. A sister shuffles over and with trembling hand sets down a cup of cappuccino. A brown puddle covers the bottom of the white saucer.

Elizabeth holds the latest edition of *The International Herald Tribune*. She bought it over on Piazza Barberini, mainly as a signal to the gregarious couple from Nova Scotia and the crude American man who chews with his mouth open that she has no interest in conversation. She wants to be alone. Little in the newspaper connects with the world she knows. Nothing about U.S. politicians or Hollywood celebrities. She reads about a coup in Burkina Faso, the draught in central China. An article tells how turtles in the Mediterranean are dying from ingesting plastics tourists leave on beaches.

Page four. "It can't be," she says so forcefully that people at nearby tables turn to look.

She adjusts her glasses, thrusts the newspaper at arm's length. Same hair, same dress even. And no legs. But in the photo she no longer has Mary's eyes; the child's are dull, without emotion.

Most likely the newspaper identifies her as an accomplice to numerous thefts. But no. "While Italian officials insist the government has made great strides in providing suitable living conditions for the Romani, health officials are bringing the real conditions to the public's attention." The Romani camp where Tsura lives, the paper reports, is on the site of a former toxic waste dump. Years ago the government declared the site safe for a camp, but the ground water is contaminated with arsenic, lead, and heavy metals. The Romani are suffering from still births and birth defects, yet the government and the chemical company refuse to acknowledge the problem.

A frog in the farm pond. An amphibian. Now a child. A human child.

AS SOON AS SHE'S SWALLOWED the last sip of coffee, Elizabeth exits the doorway watched over by the alabaster Mary. She passes the convent office where two sisters seem to be arguing over something related to a computer problem, then descends outdoor steps to the courtyard. In the courtyard's center a wrought iron bench overlooks a three-tiered fountain. She sits and closes her eyes, absorbed in the song of the fountain's gentle splashes. Until she notices, in the distance, the rumbling traffic of Piazza Barberini. People waiting to cross the street and the man who sells newspapers from an open stall, they all inhale the exhaust. But here in this walled-off space, delicate pink blossoms emit a sweet fragrance. Hidden in trees and bushes, birds broadcast their morning songs.

Oh, what a crazy world, she thinks, with its congestion and its oases. Yet Mary hasn't given up on it. That's surely what the eyes of the Romani girl meant. Mary's eyes. She wanted Elizabeth to know that it still matters. Life still matters. That the mission isn't over. Was it for that one brief encounter that Mary led her to Rome? If so, for what end?

Why couldn't Mary just come stand in front of her and tell her what to do? Right here, right now. Maybe she's supposed to search for Tsura. Impossible, given Elizabeth doesn't speak Italian.

She's scheduled to fly home tomorrow. Without any answers. And still without even a clear question other than *what next?* There's just this continued gnawing in her viscera caused by her worries about Angelica and her own future.

SHE HAS NO IDEA WHAT TO DO with the day other than to continue visiting churches. But instead of selecting them according to the map in her guide book, she locates them haphazardly, by boarding random buses. She rides around town, standing packed against other passengers, smelling their body odor, hearing their wheezes. To anticipate where to get off, she peers out windows by leaning over those who are seated. Moments ago a man cleared his throat, a signal that her breast was in his face.

Through the bus window she spots a church. Exits at the next stop and walks back.

Ahead of her a man in suit and tie enters the open door, followed by a woman wearing chic teal pants and blouse. As if a microphone has been placed on the stone floor, the clanks of the woman's high heels echo, along with the scraping somewhere of a moved chair. For a while Elizabeth stands at the back, next to a rack of materials requesting a donation for necessary restorations.

A narrow doorway is to her right. She steps through it into a small chapel lit only by the glow of votive candles along a table. Behind the altar hangs an oil painting of Mary, arms outstretched, face turned heavenward. Reminding Elizabeth of the Brothers' song, "This world is not my home." Yet she's confident that Mary is not detached, she does indeed dwell among humans. On Planet Earth, which she cares about.

Elizabeth takes a seat on the second of six rows.

*How did I get here? In a city that is foreign yet familiar, crowded yet intimate, searching for one who is with me yet has abandoned me? And why has Daddy so often intruded?*

A woman enters the chapel, puts coins in a box, and lights a candle. She kneels nearby. As Elizabeth turns slightly, she sees tears streaming down the woman's cheeks. Though it's early fall, warm still, the woman wears clothes more suited to winter: a long skirt of dark muted shades and a plaid wool jacket that doesn't match.

The words she mumbles sound like a supplication, carrying intense sadness. "O piissima Virgo Maria...tua implorantem...Virgo Virginum, Mater...verba mea...Amen."

Elizabeth rises and steps over to kneel beside her.

From somewhere an imperceptible breeze causes the candles to flutter. For what does the woman pray? For food and shelter? For her child? For her husband? For her eternal soul? Elizabeth reaches over and places a hand on the woman's shoulder, praying that her supplication will be answered. *Gratsie,* the woman whispers. She stands and leaves the chapel.

Elizabeth remains, still kneeling. Her knees ache, but she pushes the discomfort from her mind, much as one pushes aside hunger pangs. She stares into a candle, watching its flame grow longer then shorter, all the time swaying to air's invisible rhythm. How sensitive it is to its surroundings. She continues to study the votive flames, her eyes going up and down the rows of candles, each one symbolizing a prayer, most of them uttered by women. As she stares the flames unite, becoming one vast tongue of fire.

To Elizabeth's left a form emerges from the shadows. The single orange flame casts its glow on the curves of the body. It looks familiar: rounded stomach, ample breasts, heavy thighs.

"Step closer," she whispers, "so that I may see you clearly." The figure begins to dance. It is a dance more awkward than graceful, but a dance from the heart, it would seem from the way the form lifts one arm above her head and sways her hips. Around and around she twirls, moving toward Elizabeth. Mary? The figure comes out of a twirl and stops.

Elizabeth stares into her own face.

# Chapter 17

A T 35,000 FEET ABOVE THE ATLANTIC she rests her neck against an inflatable pillow. The baby two rows back has stopped crying. The young man next to Elizabeth taps his fingers in time to music on headphones handed out at the beginning of the flight.

"Listen," a familiar voice says. Her inclination is to flee, *Go to your room* long ago became her mantra. Why here? Why now?

"Listen."

*Daddy?*

"I want you to understand."

*Understand, that's what I've spent my whole life doing, trying to understand. Understand God, understand my father, understand God my father, understand God, father of us all. But God does not want—*

"You're not listening. You wanted me to be happy. I know that. You assumed all I had to do was try harder, that happiness was a matter of choice."

*Couldn't you have—*

"What is the geography of a life?" Vernon asks. "Not hills and valleys—those are easy to discern—but the crevasses of the mind you don't think you'll ever have the courage to climb out of."

*Quite the poet you've become. So what is it you want me to understand?*

"The power of fear."

*Fear of what?*

"I feared the world. And you."

*You were afraid of me?*

"Your curiosity. On this side I see that your questions tempted me to question as well. I thought that if I yielded, I'd lose my faith and the fellowship. I'd lose God."

*And the world? You said the world frightened you too.*

"The Brothers' strict rules about what's right and what's wrong gave me a sense of security and confidence. To be *of the world* would have required me to see pain and injustice. I was scared by what I might see, more so by what might be required of me."

*You saw no reason to argue with the Brothers? When they taught that man is God's glory, could you not argue that the fox and the groundhog and the ant and the ladybug are also God's creation and worthy of honor? When the Brothers insisted that God created everything for man's use—dominion over all the Earth, they preached—why couldn't you confront them?*

"That's my point, Elizabeth. I was controlled by fear. I lacked the courage to argue on behalf of God's world. My cowardice made me sad. Always sad. You must seek the courage."

ON THE FINAL LEG OF HER RETURN HOME, between New York and Knoxville, the man in the aisle seat is forced to bend his huge frame as if trying to fit into an envelope. There is no room for the tray to come down, and the breadth of his shoulders presses her against the window. In spite of her discomfort she must have dozed off. When she opens her eyes, the plane has begun its descent. The flight attendants walk the aisle picking up plastic cups and napkins imprinted with the airline's logo.

She gazes out the window, down at the earth below. Her astonishment is audible, a low moan that causes the man beside her to turn toward her. The descent has brought into view, not her mountains, not the forested ridges with their gently sloping peaks. These might as well be on the moon, for instead of rising toward the heavens, they are open sores, ashen gray craters bordered by steep ashen gray walls. Ashen gray roads wind within the shredded landscape. Yellow machines move around as if they are robots operating according to their own rules. Chewing up the land, spitting it over the edge to fill valleys and streams.

A child who lives on land that was once a toxic waste dump, a frog with an extra leg growing from its abdomen. And now mountain tops hospitable to neither fox nor oak tree, land that can never again be as Creator intended it. The reality of the future grabs her gut. Twists it. A future in which all of Earth will resemble this spot, so exploited by humans that little, if anything, will remain of Eden.

It comes on her so quickly that she barely has a chance to reach for the folded white bag. She vomits.

"God damn," the scrunched up man beside her says.

"Yes," she repeats weakly. "God damn."

HANK WASTED NO TIME in tearing down the makeshift bathhouse. The slope leading to the pond is freshly mowed. Even though it's October, patches of new green grass are starting to peek through the brown thatch where tents covered the ground. Ghosts are everywhere. Women running between tents and bathhouse in their robes. Seated around tables in the yard, laughing boisterously, eating bread prepared by Mary and Elizabeth, and the dishes each brought to share. Specters gather on the hillside on blankets and lawn chairs in anticipation of an appearance. The farm, for more than two years the center of activity and excitement, is deserted. Except for ghosts.

Traveling by herself in a foreign country for ten days, surrounded by a language she couldn't understand, being hosted by disinterested, even hostile, nuns—all those factors combined are nothing compared to the degree of isolation she now feels. Maybe, before she does anything more, she should go get Jezebel at Hank's. Create her own welcoming committee. But Hank's wife will take her captive and insist on hearing in detail about every Italian dish Elizabeth ate.

She considers calling someone from among her circle of friends, one of the women who used to get together on Sunday evenings. But Mary's appearances ended up straining those relationships.

A reminder that friendship is fickle. She spent her college years so desperate for friends that she eagerly tailored herself to be accepted by the unacceptables. Only to discover that she had no value beyond satisfying their need to feel powerful. Get her drunk. Screw her. Discard her. "Blest be the tie that binds," the Sisters sang, which Elizabeth believed included her. Only to discover that she had no value beyond satisfying their need to feel more pious, more right with the Lord.

Who does she have left? Not even Mary and Angelica.

The house offers no more cheer than the grounds. Streams of light from the west window create dust sparkles in the air. She fluffs a pillow on the sofa, straightens the corner of the area rug. She runs her hand across the kitchen counter, once crowded with women's potluck contributions.

Her hand comes to rest on a stack of unopened mail Hank must have put there. Next to a loaf of fresh bread. Just when she's been despairing over human relationships, this kind man has made sure she has something to eat upon her arrival. She carries the mail over to the kitchen table and takes a seat. Bills, advertisements. Several thank-you notes from women who found strength or comfort in their Willow Pond Farm experience.

Stuck in the middle of the pile, a plain business envelope with no stamp, no return address. Her heart does a somersault. She recognizes the ease with which the writer held the pen, the feminine slant of the letters. She rips open the envelope.

Dear Mom,

I just learned that someone in our group is heading your way and is willing to drop off a letter. I received two of your emails from Rome. I don't quite get why you went there, but you're more attuned to Mary's ways than I. I hope you found what you went for.

I'm sorry to cause you so much worry. You are in my heart, as I am in yours.

Because of our close bond I need you to understand why I'm taking such radical action. If I stayed with my studies, despair over the future of the planet would consume me. You might say I'm choosing hope over despair. The only way to feel hopeful is to do something. Change will come.

You may recognize the church's influence in my decision. I have taken the idea of discipleship to heart and am willing to die for the cause. So you see I recognize the danger I face. But what greater privilege can there be than to risk one's life for a cause greater than self? Of what value is a life devoted to self-interest and a consumer lifestyle that threatens to destroy God's creation? And look at it this way: with your gift, if/when I'm on the other side, we'll be in touch.

Mom, I'm able to follow this course because of you. You represent the courage it takes to pay attention to the voices and forces that speak to you. Thank you for modeling that courage for me.

I love you.

Angelica

P.S. Each day is filled with hours of inaction and I have time to think. All this is the result of my musings.

A RED AND WHITE QUILT COVERS the double bed with its sagging mattress. Above the bed hangs a framed picture of the willow tree and pond, painted by a local artist after she came to several of Mary's appearances. Personal touches claim this room as Elizabeth's space: her meditation table with geode and candle atop Cloth of Terra. On the battered chest of drawers are photos of Randy and Angelica as children, one with their arms around each other, laughing.

She tosses her suitcase on the bed and begins to unpack. Carries her cosmetic case across the hall to the bathroom, drops the Guatemalan dress, navy blue pants, and tops in the clothes hamper. At the bottom of the suitcase rests a thin stack of papers, one the folded newspaper with the article about Tsura.

Elizabeth pushes the suitcase aside and stretches across the bed to study the picture. A little girl loved by her mother. As Elizabeth loves her children. Even though Randy hates her, she clings to memories of a little boy who held her hand as they searched for wild raspberries. Maybe someday he'll remember too and recognize that she did the best she could.

Tsura's mother. What are her memories? Where is her hope? Surely her heart aches for this child with dull eyes and missing limbs. Maybe Tsura's mother has already died from the poisons and the girl has been left in the care of her older sister.

Elizabeth's eyes wander back to the pictures on the chest of drawers. To one in particular, of Angelica when she was four. The sun glistening on her auburn hair, a bright green leaf resting in her palm, she smiles into the camera. A happy girl growing up on a farm near a small American town. A safe town, a healthy town.

Tsura, also a child, lives in a camp on top of a former toxic dump, drinking water from the well. Born to a woman who has breathed the same air and drunk the same water. How many other children and pregnant women live there?

"Mother of God! What can be done?"

IT HAS BEEN AN EXHAUSTING DAY, begun in Rome, ending here, almost 5,000 miles away. In Italy it's four in the morning, so she should fall asleep easily. But she can't. Lying first on her back, then on her stomach, then on her back, she has no control over her mind, which darts from Angelica to little Tsura. Back to Angelica. Back to Tsura.

How long this unrest lasts, she doesn't know. She awakens to blackness shrouding everything. Quite different from Rome, where city lights brighten the sky all night long.

She puts on robe and slippers and wraps herself in the quilt. Goes downstairs. She's hungry and intends to make a bowl of oatmeal. Instead, as if sleep walking, she passes through the kitchen, steps out onto the stoop, into the night. A chill penetrates the air, but she's impervious to temperature as she makes her way down to the pond. Near the water's edge, she lies on the ground, gazing upward.

Above, the Milky Way arcs across the sky. Over the great expanse millions of individual stars flicker. She locates Arcturus to her right, Vega, almost straight overhead. Polaris. From the multitude of stars those are the only ones she can identify. Astronomers, she's sure, recognize many others.

"Tsura," she whispers. What a difference it makes to know a child's name. The photos of children in Sudan and Ethiopia, in Sao Paulo, and Port-au-Prince—like the stars overhead, their names are unknown to her. A farmer she knew up in Virginia wouldn't let his family name any of the animals because he didn't want to upset the children at butchering time.

When stars or animals or people have names, they matter more. Polar bears disappearing from the Arctic. Sad, but she knows no polar bear by name. The Bengal tiger is disappearing. Sad, but she knows no Bengal tiger by name either.

Listen to Willow. Listen to Toad. Listen to Wind.

....Listen to Earth.

"I am a child of Creator," she hears as she lies by the pond, "born of love, blessed with beauty." A sigh, like the shudder of a barely perceptible earthquake. The faint sound of sobbing. Through the damp grass, through the layers of soil and rock, her body feels Earth's heartbeat, the deep ache of violation. Unafraid of bears and raccoons that regularly pass through, she falls asleep.

A GENTLE SUN PEEKING over the mountain awakens her. She expects Jezebel to come lick her face. No, Jezebel's still at Hank's.

Elizabeth's chilled body complains about having slept on the ground. She rolls onto her side and pushes herself to a half-sitting position. Gradually she's able to stand, stretch, restore a measure of flexibility to shoulders and spine.

She looks toward the garden. The summer apprentices' return to college has permitted decay's gradual takeover. In the orchard a few apples still cling to trees. In the woodland beyond, leaves have already faded to a dull green. Soon they will be falling to the ground, rotting. Not so much dust to dust, ashes to ashes, as beauty to compost. Having burst forth in the spring, bright green against an azure sky, they have run their course.

Her own life coming to an end before long too. She considers her body with its aching joints, its sagging breasts and fleshy arms. Not a young woman's body, to be sure. Not even a middle-aged woman's. What's she to do about her attachment to this corporal existence?

To stay here on the farm, to run the business and hike nearby trails seem a way of avoiding responsibility to—to what? Angelica? To Earth itself?

Wrapped in the quilt she walks to the pond's edge. Squats to scoop up water, splashes it on her face. It dribbles down her chin, drips onto her neck, slides between her breasts. She shivers. Yet she reaches for more water. Pouring a handful over her head, she closes her eyes as its chill runs down her face. She drops the quilt, takes off robe and slippers, and lifts her nightgown over her head. Naked, she wades through the grasses at the pond's edge then pushes her toes into the muddy bottom to do a shallow dive. She feels the shock of the frigid water. She brings her face to the surface.

Always a little fearful of water, she has never permitted herself to simply be in it, trust it not to surge up her nose and send her into paroxysms of coughing. Listen to Water, Mary instructed the women. Water tells Elizabeth to relax.

With smooth strokes she swims to the center of the pond and dives into its deepest, darkest part. For two years she's been sheltered, like a child of Mary, nurtured in Mary's womb. She wonders, has the time of birth arrived? A push through the canal to commence—commence what? Elizabeth thrusts her head upward, inhaling deeply when her face reaches the surface.

Life lived backwards, she thinks. Thoughts of death preceding thoughts of birth. Where is all this leading?

At the top of the slope, Mama Bear pauses to acknowledge her then resumes a lumbering gait toward the forest

THE STORE IS EERILY QUIET. The fluorescent lights flicker, their hum interrupts the silence. Though Elizabeth enters to get granola to mix with her oatmeal, she can't help but walk up and down the aisles touching bags of whole wheat flour, honey, molasses, safflower oil. A familiar space, a business venture that testifies to her competence.

"What woman does not wish to protect that which is dear to her?" Mary Surratt whispers.

*You mean your son, your daughter, the South?*

"The songs of mockingbirds and wood thrushes, of sparrows and chickadees still ring in my head. The sweet scent of honeysuckle, the caustic odor of tobacco in the barn. You would have your daughter risk her life to protect the land while saving your own?"

Elizabeth takes the bag of granola from the shelf and turns off the light.

OPPOSING THOUGHTS SWIRL in her head: a desire to do what she can to stop the plunder of Earth and the poisoning of its creatures; a strong emotional tug to stay on the farm; confidence now is the time to take bold action; hope that it isn't.

From the pile of mail on the table, she reaches for a fund-raising request from the local food bank. She turns the envelope over and writes:

**Possibilities**
chain myself to White House fence
join Peace Corps
demonstrate outside School of the Americas (does not war destroy environment?)
help preserve jungles of Brazil (by becoming a tree-sitter?)
volunteer for World Wildlife Fund
volunteer for Sierra Club
organize a vigil at the power plant

**Reasons not to**
death
some options—affiliation w/ well-behaved people not likely to help cause
probably given job of stuffing envelopes to raise money or make telephone calls
death
can't speak Portuguese or Spanish or any other language
no access to toilets if outdoors
get shot, hanged, poisoned, bit by mosquitoes
inadequate medical care in out-of-the-way places
death

THE LAST CONSIDERATION, DEATH, tugs at her the hardest. But can she base her decisions on fear? Angelica has expressed a willingness—the desire, even—yes, Angelica *wants* to sacrifice her life for the sins of the world.

# A Vision

*Thou preparest a table before me in the presence of mine enemies. Thou preparest a table before me in the presence... Could I allow my sons to risk their lives for the independence of our beloved South and remain unwilling to do the same? Johnny argued it was men's work, not suitable for a woman. I was as committed as he, I told him. Wilkes agreed with me. Beyond suspicion he said, a respectable woman such as I. At what point does a woman step from compliance to courage? When in the core of her being she becomes aware of a terrible wrong. Thou preparest a table before me in the presence of mine enemies. Thou prepares...*

# Chapter 18

INCENSE BURNS, HANGING CRYSTALS glitter in sunlight streaming through the front window. Soothing flute music from a small CD player accompanies the gurgle of water overflowing a pottery jar and emptying into a bowl. The Garden of Hesperides bombards the senses.

Dressed in black, Betsy Padgett sits on a stool behind the counter, the glass case beneath her elbows filled with amulets and talismans. She's an attractive woman, in her late fifties, with a hint of makeup. A wide swath of shoulder-length salt and pepper hair drapes over her left eye, leaving one to wonder about the skewed world she must see. The uncovered brown eye peers from behind wire-rimmed glasses.

Betsy too, Elizabeth believes, is attuned to forces that cannot be explained. Which is why she seeks the counsel of this Crystal Resonance Therapist, purveyor of banned merchandise at Mary's appearances.

"Elizabeth," Betsy says enthusiastically, "it's so good to see you."

All the way to Asheville Elizabeth rehearsed what she planned to say. It seemed important to appear in control of her emotions and organized. But right away she starts sneezing—because of the incense—and the words spill out, not the way she intended, more like a word jumble.

"My life's falling apart. My heart's broken, I want to make my life—what's left of it—losing Mary and Angelica, the way they've both left me, and I don't know what to do now. I want to make it count for something, but I—I—I'm a coward, that's what I am. Angelica, my sweet Angelica, she's so brave. Foolishly brave, if you ask me. I don't want her to die, and I don't want to die."

Betsy's wide band of silver bracelets jangle as she reaches across the counter to clasp both of Elizabeth's hands. "Let's talk in the back, over a cup of tea." She turns the sign on the door to *Closed* and leads Elizabeth through a beaded curtain into a storage area. Two Siamese cats simultaneously jump from the ledge of the room's only window.

Shelves cluttered with inventory line the walls. A small drop-leaf table and two ladder-back chairs occupy the only cleared space. At a narrow counter, Betsy pauses to turn on a hotpot.

"Now, slower, Sugar." She nods for Elizabeth to take a seat. "What's got you so riled up?"

Elizabeth takes a deep breath. "Well, Mary left, as you know. Angelica, she took what Mary said too seriously, and she's gone too. I'm worried that the group she joined may be involved in that attack on mountaintop removal equipment up in West Virginia."

"Whew! Sabotage. I'd be worried too."

"And these, these—things just keep happening." Elizabeth tells about her search for Mary in Rome and the encounter with Tsura. The frog in her pond. About the spinning woman in Rome with Elizabeth's face.

"Mary, it's like she—she doesn't come and tell me directly, just keeps putting these things—it's like she wants me to trip over them so I'll do something."

"What do you think she has in mind?"

"I'm not sure. I think she's not going to tell me exactly. Like I'm supposed to decide on my own—to—I think she wants me to carry out her mission." Elizabeth sits quietly for a moment, her breath coming out in heavy sighs. "I'm afraid."

"Of what?"

"Of death." There. She'd said it out loud.

"I keep thinking about Angelica, how young she is. All the things she has to look forward to. While I'm—I've lived most of my life. It's a terrible thing for a mother to admit, but I'm as scared of my own death as I am of hers." She makes a slight attempt at levity: "Based on my limited experience with the dead, I doubt that walking the earth *ad infinitum* is available to the general public. Or desirable, for that matter."

Betsy doesn't smile. Her attention seems to center on stirring the tea, watching the way her spoon forms swirls. "You're not going to hot-wire bulldozers and send them over cliffs, I assume," she finally says. "Or blow up a dam. Or, or…kill anyone. Are you?"

"No, I'd never—"

"Purpose. It sounds like that's what you're struggling with. It's not just about Angelica, how much you love her, but how you're going to—how to make the years we have left matter, that's what you're talking about, isn't it?"

A few feet away one of the cats stares up at the guest, its almond-shaped blue eyes signaling that it understands human angst. Whether for its own satisfaction or to console Elizabeth, it approaches and demands in a rasping mew that she reach down and rub behind its ears.

The other cat jumps onto Betsy's lap. "I want to share something." Her bracelets clang as she vigorously strokes the cat's lean body. "Right before I turned fifty I was diagnosed with breast cancer. The big C, it gets you thinking, and I thought, well, we all die. I'm making a lot of money working for a corporation, but I'm doing nothing of value for anyone except the stockholders. So I asked myself, what are my gifts? How can I make a difference in the lives of women? I finally decided to cash in my stock options and start this little business."

She brushes aside the swath of hair hanging over her eye so that briefly she peers at Elizabeth through both lenses of her glasses. "From what I've observed you've become a stronger woman, a wiser woman. Maybe it's because Mary chose you, or maybe because you had it all along, and she recognized it. Maybe she knows you're ready. It sounds like she's giving you a shove. But you can't depend on her or anyone else to tell you what to do. You're the one who has to decide."

Both cats, one at Elizabeth's feet, the other on Betsy's lap, join Betsy in looking directly into Elizabeth's face. From the other side of the beaded curtain come the sound of flute music and the gurgle of overflowing water.

~~~
~~~

ELIZABETH SITS AT HER COMPUTER in her store office, carefully studying the websites of environmental groups. There are dozens. Some appear to be passionate in viewpoint but moderate in approach; others promote extreme measures to protect the environment (without saying what exactly those might be); still others advocate the destruction of property but not of humans or animals. Except for the tamest of the lot, they offer no contact links.

She has to trust Angelica's judgment yet be cautious. She'll include misinformation that Angelica alone will catch yet derive hidden meanings from. If by chance the wrong parties read the communication, they come away clueless. She'll begin with chatter.

To: wl83@torbox3.onion                    Oct 9  9:34 PM
Subject: Hello
Dear One,


I just want you to know that I'm back home. The farm's deserted. The appearances have ended. The summer interns have gone back to school, and I haven't reopened the store yet. Up on the ridges leaves are starting to turn. All in all, everything's sort of gloomy here. I don't quite know what to do with myself.


I hope you're having a good time. I envy your getting to camp and see much of the country. It's what I want to get around to someday soon, I'm ready to be free from business worries.


I've been reminiscing lately, thinking about our playing music together, you on the violin, me accompanying you on the piano. We got along in the store together too. We're a good team. Maybe we can work alongside each other again soon. Just say the word.


I love you.
Mom

Angelica played the trombone all through school. Other than Chopsticks, Elizabeth can't play the piano. She's never owned one.

JEZEBEL BARKS FEROCIOUSLY. Holding firmly to her collar Elizabeth opens the front door. Nearby an engine idles. Though the mail box is down at the road, Agnes Mathews has pulled into the driveway. In her blue U.S. Postal Service uniform she stands at the door, an envelope in hand.

"Strangest thing," she says. "I was at the post office this morning, just getting ready to climb into my truck, when a kid comes by on a bicycle and puts this in my hand. Said, 'A man just paid me ten dollars to give this to you. You're supposed to take it to the lady who lives at this address.'" Agnes squats to pat Jezebel. "There, girl, you know me. We're friends." She stands again. "I tell the kid it's not legal, but before I can hand it back to him he's done run off. Don't tell nobody, but since I come by here anyways, I'll go ahead and give it to you. I thought I knew just about everybody in these parts, but I swear I've never seen that kid before. You tell whoever sent it next time they have to put a stamp on their letter. The U.S. Postal Service doesn't like to be taken advantage of." A smile breaks through her scowl. "Have a good day."

She takes long strides over to the little white truck in the driveway.

Dear Elizabeth,

For reasons that will become clear, I am contacting you through unconventional channels. Your daughter has spoken to me, and she thinks that our group would benefit from having a mature woman like you join us.

If you would like to become part of our effort, please join the tour of the Thomas Wolfe House in Asheville, on November 14, at 4:00 p.m. Carry a backpack with essential clothes (including long underwear and a warm jacket) and personal items. Be prepared to be away from home three or four months.

I assume you are aware of the risks and are willing to take them.
Green Giant

THE THOMAS WOLFE HOUSE is a sprawling yellow structure with multiple additions, two stories—possibly a third, if you count what appears to be attic space—built in the Queen Anne style. Brick chimneys jut from varied roof lines, bay windows are stacked atop the other. Two rows of rocking chairs are lined up across the wide wrap-around front porch.

"The house was built in 1883," the docent says to the small group gathered at the front door. "For his daughter Cordelia, who married W.W. Barnard, who…" She speaks energetically, an apparent effort to nurture shared enthusiasm among her listeners. Already Elizabeth's shoulders ache under the weight of the backpack.

All these years she's feared she's crazy. This surely proves it. Volunteering for some absurd—she has no idea what kind of situation she's put herself in. What if fanatics got ahold of Angelica and brainwashed her? But that's what the times call for: extremists willing to act. They can change the course of history. No, at Elizabeth's age this *is* crazy. Absolutely crazy.

There's still time to back out. Nothing wrong with admitting she lacks the energy of youth. She could call Betsy to come pick her up. No, it would be letting Angelica down. And letting herself down. Angelica, though, might actually be relieved. Who wants an old hanger-on who hasn't the foggiest idea…?

"Julia Wolfe," she hears, "…an entrepreneur…Thomas Wolfe…*Look Homeward, Angel.*" She studies the other members of the tour. Who's her contact? To which one will she say, "Sorry, but I've changed my mind." Not the white mother whose teenage daughter walks ten paces behind the group with her arms defiantly folded across her chest. Not the daughter either. Not the African-American couple who appear to be on their honeymoon. Of course, they might be faking their affection, but

Elizabeth doubts it. The white man in a suit and tie who looks to be about her age, he's probably in town for business. Surely neither of the two well dressed women weighted down with expensive jewelry. Has she closed up the house and again sent Jezebel off to Hank's for nothing? Maybe somebody led her here as a joke, and Angelica doesn't even know.

"That concludes our tour." Elizabeth realizes that the group has returned to the front door. She vaguely recalls a room with an iron bed frame, where Wolfe's father died, and tables set for a meal in the bright dining room. The docent holds the door open, indicating that everyone's to exit.

She places a hand on Elizabeth's arm, as if to restrain her. "If you'll wait just a moment."

The door closes. The docent says nothing as Elizabeth nervously picks at a thread on the sleeve of her sweater. When outside conversation and the clatter of feet on the porch can no longer be heard, the docent opens the door and with a wave of the hand motions that Elizabeth is to leave.

As she steps out onto the front porch, the door closes and locks behind her.

# A Vision

*Thou preparest a table before me in the presence of mine enemies. Mine enemies. How did it come to this, that I find myself living among the enemy aggressor? That my neighbors are the perpetrators of injustice? I have read the Washington papers, filled with slander against the South and our way of life. The abolitionists betray their own race, lamenting the plight of the poor beasts of the field. Yankee politicians, trying to sound righteous, speak out for their own puffery. Should I stand idly by as Goliath boasts of his prowess? If we, the oppressed, win independence, Wilkes and I will be among the honored; if the oppressor is victorious, to them we will be known as traitors. Love thy enemies. Do good to those who curse you. Did not Aunt Rachel herself testify that I fed Union troops and cared for their horses? Northern industrialists—they call themselves Christians—they want their cotton cheap so they can sell at great profit. Is greed a Christian value? Do Christians incite the Negroes to murder their masters and set fire to their homes? Do Christians arrogantly disrupt the lives of people living a peaceful existence? Listen, Elizabeth, a woman must do all she can so that justice will prevail. Thou preparest a table before me in the presence of mine enemies. Thou preparest...*

# Chapter 19

A DARK BLUE 1988 IMPALA covered with rust pockmarks comes to a halt in front of the Thomas Wolfe house. From the front passenger side a young white woman unfolds her daddy-longlegs body and gets out to open the door to the backseat. She nods to Elizabeth, an invitation it seems. Elizabeth removes the backpack from her shoulders and slides across ripped blue vinyl. The young woman gets in beside her. No words are exchanged.

Where's Angelica? Is it too soon to ask? Elizabeth decides to wait. Let the driver and the woman take the initiative in conversation.

The car pulls away from the curb, makes its way along side streets. In unhurried fashion the driver slows at traffic lights, stops to allow pedestrians to cross. He's hunched intently over the steering wheel, his dark curly hair peeking out of an Atlanta Braves baseball cap turned backward. A handsome face the shade of a copper penny, Elizabeth can see in the rearview mirror, with a little beard growth and bushy eyebrows. A small hoop earring in his right ear. He's probably about Angelica's age, mid-twenties. Once when their glances meet, his brown eyes smile at her. Not the eyes of a terrorist. On the other hand, when not meeting her gaze, his nervously dart about, hyper-alert. What makes her think she can recognize a terrorist's eyes anyway?

"Welcome to EON," the woman beside her finally says. "That is Palmetto driving and I am Trillium. Waterlily will be at our destination. We did not want to bring her where she might be recognized." So clear is Trillium's enunciation that Elizabeth can't decide whether she's from up North or assumes the new passenger, being older, has a hearing loss.

"Waterlily?"

"Your contact." Which must mean Angelica. A relief. "I chose the name Tigerlily for you. If that is all right."

Trillium's gangly arms are draped across her lap, her long legs pushed against the front seat. Blondish hair pulled back in a ponytail and melancholy blue eyes give an appearance no more fierce than that of the young man.

"EON?" Elizabeth asks.

"Environmental Operations Network."

"Who's in it, if I may ask?"

In the driver's seat Palmetto shrugs. "Who knows?"

"Is it a big group?"

He shrugs his shoulders again. "Who knows?"

Who knows? Someone has to. "Well, who's in charge?" Elizabeth demands.

A third shrug. "Nobody."

No chairperson? No board? Isn't there someone who coordinates activities?

"Look, we do not have conventions," Trillium says, "if that is what you are thinking. No monthly newsletter. No spokesperson. It is safer that way."

Palmetto's eyes meet Elizabeth's in the rearview mirror. "We're organized into small cadres, all of them independent. We identify the part of the environmental crisis we feel most strongly about, find likeminded people, and set about taking some sort of action."

"That way," Trillium says, "no one can implicate anyone outside the cadre."

"Also why we don't use our real names."

The conversation seems to have ended. Leaving Elizabeth to contemplate the word *cadre.* Does it not imply a revolutionary organization? Something to do with communists or Mao or guns and tanks, which in turn reminds her she has no idea what kind of organization she's getting involved with. But she trusts Angelica, and looking at Trillium and Palmetto she gets the impression that these are not violent people. Or is she naive? You can't size somebody up based on physical attributes. Khrushchev, for example. He looked like a jolly old man.

Her own appearance. A harmless older woman, a casual observer would assume. Not knowing she's signed on to a venture that might reveal otherwise.

Once they're on I-40 Elizabeth tries to keep track of the route the car follows, at the same time taking fleeting glances at Trillium and Palmetto, noting their youthfulness, their intensity marked by furrowed brows and pursed lips. Perhaps Mary made a mistake assuming women's concern for their children's and grandchildren's future would inspire them to join forces to save the planet. Angelica—and now Palmetto and Trillium, all three of them young—they share the kind of passion that drastic change requires.

These almost-organized thoughts are interrupted by a fearful reminder that she's in unfamiliar territory. Not unfamiliar in geographic terms, but riding in an old Impala with two strangers, setting out on a mission she has neither knowledge of nor control over. Yet a sense of excitement surges through her body. The adrenalin rush, the rapid heart beat, the memory of another trip more than a decade ago when she drove down Route 11 toward an unknown destination.

Since the car exited I-40 darkness has fallen, and she's lost all sense of where they are. The roads winding around mountains have grown narrower. Probably half an hour has passed since they encountered another car.

Now Palmetto turns into a gravel lane barely wide enough for a single vehicle. As the car dips in and out of ruts, its axles scrape the ground. Tree branches slap against the sides.

The car comes to a stop. In that brief moment before the ignition is turned off, the headlights reveal a rundown frame house. Then all is again shrouded in darkness. The car door groans as Trillium opens it. The dim overhead light comes on, casting a yellowish hue over the torn vinyl seats. Nearby an owl screeches. A lantern's bouncing beam penetrates the night. Drawing closer, its glow waves from driver to passengers.

"M-m-Tigerlily?"

The vinyl seat squeaks as Elizabeth slides across it. Within seconds she's hugging Angelica with so much fervor that

Palmetto bolts out of the car and grabs the lantern from Angelica's hands.

"Hey, let's not burn down the whole fucking forest before our work even gets off the ground."

"Okay, okay," Elizabeth mutters under her breath.

She has no idea what lies ahead. She must wait for instructions. Isn't that how covert operations work? Each member assigned a responsibility she or he is most qualified to execute. She's here, she believes, not only because Angelica desires her presence but also because Angelica sees a role for her. Some specialized skill or quality that will help rescue Earth.

STACKED ROCK SLABS FORM steps leading up to the porch. Nearby discarded rotten board planks resemble pick-up sticks. Elizabeth holds the lantern now, lifting it high while Trillium, Palmetto, and Angelica cautiously climb the wobbly rocks. Carrying boxes from the trunk of the car, the three weave their way across the porch, then disappear into the house.

Elizabeth imagines her picture on a Hallmark card: a woman standing in the dark forest lifting a dim lantern, revealing the way—the way to what? Dozens of questions cross her mind, but she senses now's not the time to probe. Not the time to ask, what is their project? Something to do with water, but what exactly?

Yet parts of this situation have become apparent. First, they are in a remote area of either Tennessee or North Carolina. Second, the house was long ago abandoned.

Palmetto comes up behind her and takes the lantern from her hand. "Trunk's empty," he says. "Better let me carry this."

At the same time, Angelica lifts Elizabeth's backpack and takes her by the elbow. An action Elizabeth interprets as overprotective. Elizabeth withdraws her arm, reaches for the backpack, and slings it over her shoulder.

She climbs the improvised steps, adjusting her weight as the rocks wobble. Once on the porch she understands why Palmetto took the lantern, why Angelica tried to help. Sections of the porch floor have rotted. As if stepping from stone to stone to cross a shallow stream, Elizabeth follows Angelica toward the front door.

There's a *crack*. Her left leg buckles as the floor collapses beneath her. She lets go of the backpack and reaches out to clutch at something. Anything. Her feet dangle above an emptiness. She hangs by her arms, her body suspended between the dark autumn night and a netherworld with unknown inhabitants. "Ouch!" she can't help but cry out. Together Angelica and Palmetto lift her.

"We shouldn't have you arriving in the dark your first time here," Palmetto says. "Are you okay?"

"I—I probably scraped some skin somewhere. Nothing serious."

Surely they're all paying close attention, assessing whether this older woman will be a help or a liability.

A stone fireplace dominates what probably once served as the parlor. A small flame casts shadows on the rough wood floor. Fragments of brittle wallpaper cling to the walls. There is no furniture.

Trillium makes a half-bow and sweeps her right arm out as if showing off the house. "Make yourself at home," she says with a trace of a giggle.

Indoors, lantern light offers a better look at Angelica. Apparently life as a—what is she? Activist? Terrorist? In either case Elizabeth worries that she looks thinner. Like Trillium she wears her hair pulled back in a pony tail. It's oily, her jeans grimy and loose.

There's someone else in the house. In the kitchen. Another man, probably in his twenties, small in stature, with skin the shade of mocha, round wire-rimmed glasses, and dreadlocks gathered in a ponytail. He greets Elizabeth with an extended hand and a slightly upturned mouth, almost a smile. Like Palmetto, he has the beginnings of a beard.

"Name's Ro-uh-Tumbleweed," he says as way of introduction.

"Tigerlily," she says, taking his hand.

Heavy black paper covers the single kitchen window. The only work surface is the ridged drying area of a cast-iron sink with disconnected pipes. On one side of the sink, a camp stove stands on metal legs, on the other side there's a closed door. Leading outside? she wonders. Narrow cupboards hang on the wall opposite the sink, their hinges rusty, their white enamel paint chipped.

Boxes carried from the car are on the floor beneath the cabinets. Tumbleweed starts to empty them. He stoops and stands, filling the cupboards with mac and cheese, cans of Chef Boyardee stew and pasta, canned tuna. Has Angelica, a vegetarian who's particular about nutrition, been eating this kind of over-salted, overcooked processed food? Quantities signal a stay of maybe a week, depending on appetites.

A square oak table stands near the window, its surface marred by water and scorch stains. Around the table there are four mismatched chairs with backs, a fifth one backless. A lit oil lamp rests on the table.

"Did you get the mouse traps?" Angelica asks Trillium.

As if she fears one will spring, Trillium cautiously reaches into a box. "Are you gonna be the one to set them?"

"Why do you think we invited my muh—Tigerlily?" Angelica winks at Elizabeth.

A narrow stairway leads up to three rooms. Elizabeth deposits her backpack in a corner of the *girls' room*. Faded scraps of wallpaper cling to wooden planks. Three sleeping bags are spread on the bare wood floor, one with a foam pad underneath.

"That one's for you," Angelica says.

Elizabeth kisses her on the cheek. "Aw, that's sweet. And the bathroom?"

"You're looking at it." Angelica points to an enamel bucket in the corner. "We go outside during the day. This is for after dark."

She places both arms on Elizabeth's shoulders. "Uh, Mom, I think we need to be aware of boundaries. Like we're not mother and daughter here so much as we're working for a common cause. You need to think of me as Waterlily. To me you're Tigerlily." She hugs Elizabeth and whispers, "We know though, don't we, that you're really my mommy?"

*Waterlily, Waterlily,* Elizabeth repeats to herself. *Not Angelica. Waterlily.*

As they turn for the door, Elizabeth asks, "So what's the plan? Everyone's so reticent."

EARLIER TRILLIUM SAID this little cadre calls itself Friends of Water. Part of EON, though EON seems to be a non-organization. From outward appearances, it's not an intimidating group. Trillium with her gangly body; Waterlilly, Elizabeth knows, so sensitive she can't tolerate the notion of killing animals for meat; Palmetto with his heart-melting brown eyes and baseball cap turned backward; Tumbleweed, whose wire-framed glasses give him the appearance of an intellectual. And now Tigerlilly.

ELIZABETH SLIPS OUT of her sleeping bag into the frigid room. The night was anything but restful. The foam pad offered little relief from the hardness of the floor, and little creatures of unknown identity scampered only a few feet from her head. *They too are part of Creation,* Mary would say. Sure, but couldn't they at least search for food in some other part of the house? Nearby, curled in their sleeping bags, Waterlilly and Trillium inhale and exhale in rhythm with each other.

With a flashlight Elizabeth locates her jeans and down jacket. She pulls away the edge of heavy black paper covering the window. Only a hint of daylight. The blackness of the surrounding forest reminds her of fairy tales she read to her children. Once upon a time. Ravenous wolves, cannibalistic witches—unknown denizens of these woods. And no bread crumbs or pebbles strewn to show the path back. Not that she wants to go home. She's committed.

All is quiet downstairs. With kindling and newspaper someone gathered, she restarts the fire. As she kneels by the fireplace, her thoughts dash as rapidly as the flame spreads from the strike of a single match to the crackle of burning newspaper to the hiss of small sticks to the sputter of larger ones. Anxiety over what lies ahead, relief over being reunited with Angelica.

Satisfaction over being involved in something that could make a difference. Pessimism that it can. Back to anxiety.

An urge to relieve herself draws her away from the fire's increasing warmth. As she suspects, the kitchen door leads outside. Behind the house what was once a cleared and tilled plot of land is now overgrown with Joe-Pye weed. A few faded pink blossoms still cling to tall stalks. The brightening sky to her left indicates the house faces north, that the cultivated plot had a southern exposure. Except for a cluster of spruce pines, the area is surrounded by dense hardwood forest. Decaying leaves on the forest floor fill the air with a moldy stench.

Trampled grass suggests a path others have taken—to an outhouse she hopes. But instead of finding one in usable condition, she comes to a narrow building leaning like a drunk. The door has creaking hinges, the seat is gone. The floor too. Only a pit remains, its contents long dried up. This may explain the fork in the path she was just following. One direction for males, one for females? Since no one else is up yet, it probably doesn't matter which she chooses. She takes the path to the right and squats behind a cluster of mountain laurel.

Returning to the clearing she sees something she didn't notice earlier. On the other side of the house, beyond the field of Joe-Pye weed, stands a small square structure of river rock, its roof of rusted tin. A door has been constructed of haphazard lengths of boards. She lifts the latch and enters. Faint light from outside reveals a cement trough. Water from a pipe flows into the trough, then out through a hole at the other end. Two gallon jugs of milk and several large glass containers are immersed in water, apparently stored there by her co—her co—whatever.

Her exploration has made her curious about the property's original inhabitants. Who was adventuresome enough to live in such an isolated place? Did they leave because they were lonely or because somebody died or because they couldn't sustain themselves on this plot of land? There's probably a grave or two nearby.

Returning to the house, she finds the others seated at the kitchen table. Her cheerful *Good morning* is met with silence. No *How did you sleep?* or *Thanks for building the fire.* Since childhood, a forced smile has been all Angelica can manage at the beginning of a day. Apparently the other three share her aversion to morning conversation.

Hair disheveled, eyes glazed over, all four wear dirty sweatshirts and jeans. Chins nearly touch chipped ceramic bowls as they scoop Cheerios into their mouths. Three grams of fiber, nutritional information on the side of the box says, not enough for a woman her age. She expresses gratitude for the cup of instant coffee Tumbleweed prepared from water heated on the camping stove, but she misses the morning java fragrance. She follows suit as they all wash their own bowl, cup, and spoon in a chipped enamel basin, then drain each item on a faded cotton dishtowel spread across the ridged drying area of the sink.

Next Waterlily and Palmetto, car key in hand, head out the front door. Without explanation of how their leaving relates to the plan. Trillium and Tumbleweed say nothing. Elizabeth wants to ask *Where are you going?* After all, she's part of this group and deserves to know what's happening. Yet she holds her tongue. Not out of trepidation but because it seems wiser just to observe for a while. Get in the rhythm.

From the kitchen window she watches them adjust their balance on the improvised stone steps of the front porch and head into the woods. Soon she hears the grinding sound of a starting engine. The Impala materializes from beyond the spruce pines then exits from view.

A THUMP! draws her attention back inside. Tumbleweed has dropped a massive book onto the kitchen table. The cover is of faded blue linen, its corners worn down to the cardboard.

"That looks like a dictionary." she says.

He looks up. Eyes behind wire-rimmed glasses appear scholarly. Is he a law student? Maybe studying for an exam to become a doctor or some other sort of professional?

"I hitchhiked here. The last guy who picked me—I had to share the seat with this poetry anthology. A hundred miles of holding it on my lap made me feel—I guess you could say the book and I developed a kinship. He sold it to me for five bucks."

"But you still had to carry it some distance, didn't you?"

He raises one shoulder to indicate a lopsided torso, and grins. "Does this answer your question?"

In the main room Trillium has taken a seat on the floor near the fireplace. Her long legs stretch out in front of her, ankles are crossed. She's reading a paperback novel with a picture of a robust man and a scantily-clad woman on the cover.

"Is there anything I can do?" Elizabeth asks.

Trillium puts the book down. "I know that feeling."

Out in the world of clean hair and clean clothes people probably stare at the beauty of this stately young woman, whose real name might be Amy or Stephanie or Kimberly. Does her mother know about her activism? Surely someone, somewhere, worries.

Trillium continues. "We have all sort of put our lives on hold. But just relax for now. It will get intense soon enough."

"Meaning what?"

"It is like fishing. You wait and wait. Once the fish takes the bait, everything changes." She picks up her book. Conversation over.

Elizabeth can think of nothing to do but sit. On the crumbling concrete step outside the back kitchen door, she absorbs the warmth of the morning sun. *Build your own relationships,* Angelica—Waterlily—said. The summer interns on the farm, they seemed to like her. But she was their boss. No, more a mentor. Here her status is ambiguous. Surely someone has written a how-to book for relationships across generational lines. She tries to conjure up its advice but can think of nothing applicable to this kind of situation other than *Don't act old.*

There's a legal pad in a pocket of her backpack. With nothing to read, she could write. Continue the chronicle of her life's journey. She fetches paper and pen and returns to the back stoop.

A little past noon Waterlily and Palmetto return. Joining the others at the kitchen table, eating potato chips and tuna sandwiches on white bread, the two continue a disagreement that must have started in the car.

"What I keep telling her—but she won't listen—is that we don't know what the fuck we're doing." Appealing for confirmation, Palmetto turns anxious eyes to Tumbleweed.

Tumbleweed, though, shrugs his shoulders and says nothing.

"Blowing up a holding dam," Palmetto continues, "would be a hell of a lot more effective."

"And I keep telling you," Waterlily says, "we have to trust our Raleigh contacts." When she crosses her arms across her chest like that, Elizabeth knows there's no budging her. "They'll do the communicating. Once the state acknowledges the study—that's our goal for now. And the public, when they see and know these guys have been withholding information, once they learn their children—"

"And what difference will that make?" Palmetto jerks the Atlanta Braves hat from his head to reveal a patch of thinning hair above his forehead. "As long as it's not my kid, that's what people think."

Trillium turns her body from the table, stretches out her legs, and looks directly at Palmetto. "If you are that pessimistic, why are you even here?"

"I just think it's going to take more drastic action. Like blowing something up. One time, that's all it will take, one time. Release sludge into a river and into some town's water supply, then people'll pay attention."

Waterlily slams her fist on the table. "I can't believe we're having this conversation again. We've already decided all this. We've got a copy of the page and intel he'll be in the area. We can't force the public to care, that's obvious. We can only expose the cover-up. It's withholding the information that damns him."

Trillium takes a bite from her sandwich. "Our contacts in Raleigh are set. Changing the plan is not an option."

POW! A SINGLE GUNSHOT interrupts forest commotion. Birds, squirrels, and other creatures suddenly stop singing and chirping. Elizabeth stands behind the house, feet apart, gripping the handle of a revolver.

"Let your left thumb rest on the right one," Tumbleweed tells her.

She lowers the pistol while he lines up five partially intact bottles they found in a rubbish heap a short distance into the forest.

"Okay, let's try again," he says. "Keep your arms straight, but don't lock them."

One at a time, she aims at the bottles. She hits the two largest ones.

"Most important of all," Tumbleweed says, "don't be afraid to use it."

# A Vision

*Yea though I walk through the valley of the shadow of death, through the…Oh, dear God, hanged! I have witnessed such events, the noose around a man's neck, the drop. A terrible way to die. I am not afraid of the hereafter, but of that moment. I will ask General McCall to place the noose—I want no stranger to do it. Anna, I need to see my daughter. And a priest. Father Wiget, Father Walter. I must be calm. For Anna's sake. Jesus, I am ready to see you face to face. Mother Mary, I am ready to see you. I will fear no evil, I will fear no evil. Johnny, I am dying for you. Southland, I am dying for you. God, I am dying for the cause you sanctified. Bless me now, dear Father, bless me, Holy Virgin. Elizabeth. Elizabeth. May the value of our lives be determined not by what we believe but by what we do to save our blessed land. Yea, though I walk through the valley…*

# Chapter 20

ARTIN BLANKTON, head of the North Carolina Department of Environment and Natural Resources, is en route to a hunting vacation at a friend's lodge in Swain County. Or so the intercepted message states. On a moonless night, a few minutes before midnight, according to plan and through the efforts of an EON contact in Raleigh, one of Blankton's tires goes flat on a remote road. In the diffused beam of the trunk light, he lifts the spare from the back of the SUV. A 1988 Impala approaches from the opposite direction. It stops. Five people get out, all wearing ski masks. Four brandish revolvers. Elizabeth, a.k.a. Tigerlily, has been designated wielder of a giant flashlight, aimed at Blankton's face. Bulging eyes behind his glasses reveal fear and confusion.

"Help!" he shouts into the deaf night, seconds before Angelica, a.k.a. Waterlily, thrusts a gun in his ribs.

While Elizabeth blinds him with a beam of light, Palmetto and Waterlily each grab an arm. They shove his short chubby frame toward the Impala. There Tumbleweed waits, in his left hand a rope, duct tape, and a kitchen towel. In his right hand, a revolver.

About two heads taller than Blankton, Trillium steps in front of him. Legs planted apart, she takes leather gloves from a pocket of her denim jacket. "Your keys, Asshole," she demands, extending a hand. Waterlily releases her hold so that Blankton can reach in his pocket. But instead of doing as he was told, he clutches a single key, pivots to his right, and with a swift upswing thrusts it toward Waterlily's face. It catches the bottom of her ski mask. The flashlight reveals a gash extending from the corner of her mouth up her cheek. She utters a startled cry and steps back in pain.

"Son of a bitch!" Palmetto yells. Still holding one arm firmly, he brings his revolver up to Blankton's temple.

Tumbleweed's reflexes are swift. He drops everything and darts to the captive's side. He grabs and twists Blankton's other arm. Too late. Somewhere in the darkness the keys land with a clink. The three men stand there in a clutch, all breathing heavily.

Waterlily holds her hand to her cheek and moans. The mask still covers most of her face.

"Over here, Tigerlily," Tumbleweed yells. "Keep the light on us."

"No, over here," Trillium orders from darkness near the car. "Find the keys!"

Elizabeth stands frozen. Her instinct is to help her daughter.

"Go, Mom," Waterlily whispers. "I'll cover the guys." She puts the revolver in one sweatshirt pocket, takes a small flashlight from another.

The racket of confrontation has abated. As if waiting for humans to exit the scene, the forest is silent. Elizabeth directs the flashlight toward Blankton's feet, shines the beam to his right, to his left. Trillium, down on hands and knees, brushes gloved hands over the road surface.

Meanwhile Palmetto and Tumbleweed bind Blankton's hands and legs with the rope, cover his eyes with a dish towel, and put duct tape over his mouth.

"Look under the car," Palmetto urges. "Hurry up. We've got to get out of here."

While Elizabeth squats, sweeping the flashlight's beam over the dark tar, Trillium crawls partway under the Impala. "Here they are."

Back on her feet she walks over to Blankton's SUV and opens the back door. Tosses a jumbo duffle bag to the ground. "Wouldn't want him to be without clean underwear," she says. In the driver's seat of his car, she starts the engine and drives into the night. Five minutes later she reappears on foot. The Impala's trunk lid closes on Blankton, lying in a fetal position.

"Strange," Trillium says from the backseat on their return to the hideout. "I looked for his gun and didn't find one. If he's going hunting, where is it?"

"Maybe the guy who owns the lodge furnishes one," Waterlily says.

"Something's not right," Trillium says.

Shortly past two a.m. the car pulls into the long narrow lane leading to the house. To avoid a repeat of someone falling through the porch floor, Tigerlily and Trillium have stomped a trail through waist-high grass along the side of the house. Now, by lantern light, Palmetto and Tumbleweed remove the binding around Blankton's legs. Still blind-folded, he is partly pulled, partly shoved to the backdoor, through the kitchen, up the stairs.

The room where he's to be held contains a sleeping bag, pee bucket, and a sagging plaid easy chair with leaking foam insides. In the middle of the floor a rusted grate fits over an opening through which heat rises from the parlor below. Heavy black paper covers the only window. The backless kitchen chair stands outside the door, there for whoever's on guard duty. Everyone but Elizabeth will take a turn. Because they assume she lacks the necessary toughness? she wonders. Does she offer this venture nothing more than holding lanterns and flashlights?

The discussion about whether Waterlily should seek medical attention in Bryson City is short. Tumbleweed takes a first-aid kit from the kitchen cupboard, cleans and bandages the wound. Going to a doctor would involve too much risk: forms to be filled out, identification provided. Besides, Elizabeth learns, Angelica doesn't have health insurance.

WITH INTERNET AND CELL PHONE reception blocked by mountains, communications with Raleigh contacts have to be made in Bryson City. Even this late in the year enough strangers come and go in the town, hunters mostly, that passersby won't likely notice two more outsiders. One male, one female. Both white. A young black man like Tumbleweed, though, may draw attention, especially if he walks alongside a white woman. He's to stay out of public view.

While Trillium and Palmetto make the trip, Tumbleweed keeps guard outside Blankton's door. A revolver rests on an upside-down bushel basket beside him. The poetry anthology rests on his lap. "Absolutely every poem ever written in the

English language," Palmetto has said of the volume, with a smirk.

While Tumbleweed reads poetry and guards Blankton, Elizabeth, a.k.a. Tigerlily, and Angelica, a.k.a. Waterlily, sit at the kitchen table, fingers grasping chipped mugs of instant coffee. Angelica has raised the black window covering to let in the small amount of brightness seeping through a dense cloud cover.

From a battery-powered radio on the floor, an announcer broadcasts local news. "No one was injured in a Macon County home fire last night. The fire department arrived on the scene…"

Elizabeth gazes outside, her eyes following two squirrels chasing each other up a tree, leaping like trapeze artists across a chasm to the limb of another tree, to another, to another, until they're out of sight.

Since arriving a week ago, she's wondered, but finally has a chance to ask Angelica: "Why did you decide to include me?" She tries not to sound like she's whining. "So far I'm only good for holding a flashlight. I'm not even included in the schedule to sit outside Blankton's room. To be honest I feel like the proverbial fifth wheel."

From the radio: "And in last night's high school football, the Eagles beat the…"

Angelica reaches across the table to grasp Elizabeth's hand. "I understand. After I read your message, the idea came to me and I couldn't let it go. I saw how Mary funneled her power through you, until I didn't know if the words were hers or yours. I figure she trusted you. I trust you too. We don't know where this—our having Blankton—who knows how this will turn out? I anticipate we're probably going to need a mature voice, your voice."

"Seems like more than maturity is needed. Organization, for example. I can't figure out who the leader is. It looks to me like everyone—I know you're committed. But why are they here, the others? Are they looking for adventure? I don't see any indication that they're passionate about the environment."

"No, you're wrong. We talked through the issues before you got here. Everybody's on board."

"And the leader?"

"We're a democratic group. We operate by consensus. You're one of us now. Your voice counts."

"I'm not sure what that means."

The slam of car doors interrupts the discussion. Footsteps cross the porch; the front door opens and closes. Elizabeth and Angelica carry their coffee mugs into the main room, where they return to being Waterlily and Tigerlily.

"All that way for nothing," Trillium groans as she and Palmetto enter. She steps to the fireplace, rubbing hands together over the sputtering logs. "Something's gone wrong. Sourwood's got the bulletin ready to go out as soon as the story breaks, but there's been no mention of it on local or national news. Nobody misses him."

"I told you guys, this ain't gonna work," Palmetto says. "We're out here in the boondocks where we've got no control over events."

"We have to trust our people in Raleigh," Waterlily says.

THE *BLANKTON SUITE,* THEY call it: the narrow upstairs room where their captor has spent his first day in the worn easy chair of faded plaid. His hands and ankles are bound with strips of an old sheet, periodically removed to allow the blood to circulate. Only nature's call allows him the freedom to move over to the pee bucket, and that with the assistance of Tumbleweed or Palmetto.

Earlier, in a lengthy discussion about sensory deprivation, Waterlily gave an impassioned speech declaring that their purpose isn't to torture Blankton but to pressure those in power to release the paper. Let him see his surroundings, she said, just not his captors.

Now the five Friends of Water, all wearing ski masks, surround Blankton in a semicircle.

"What's all this about?" Blankton demands. "What do you people want?"

A day without a shave and shower, still wearing clothes he was seized in—chinos and a plaid flannel shirt under a fleece lined jacket—he seems a pudgy caricature of a once-important man.

"Martin. May I call you Martin?" Palmetto leans menacingly toward the captive and pokes a gun in his stomach. "Here's how things stand. If I understand correctly, your agency's mission is to protect North Carolina's environment. But you haven't been protecting it, have you? You've got friends in manufacturing. You've got friends in the logging industry. You've got friends at Duke Energy—my goodness, Martin, you've got friends everywhere, it seems. So just whose environment are you protecting? Huh?"

In spite of having five masked people towering over him, his own body sunken in a deteriorated easy chair, Blankton manages a condescending tone: "Obviously you don't understand the complexity of issues we deal with. I dare say you wouldn't know how to run a lemonade stand."

"We'll see if you change your mind during your time with us," Trillium says. "By the way, don't expect anybody to trace your location through your cell phone."

"They'll find me."

"Now that's what's called wishful thinking," Tumbleweed says. "Fucking wishful thinking. Eric Rudolph, remember him? The fucker who planted a bomb at the Atlanta Olympics? He hid out in these parts for five years. Yep, it took them five years to find him."


"WE'RE GOING OUTSIDE for fun and games," Tumbleweed tells Blankton. "But I'm warning you, you got to behave. As you can see, Tigerlily here has a gun. You don't want to mess with her, you hear?"

Elizabeth, a.k.a. Tigerlily, isn't sure whether he's serious or joking. In either case she nudges Blankton's arm with the gun muzzle.

"I repeat, you hear?"

Blankton lifts his chin at a belligerent angle. "Yeah, I hear."

"Inside you can yell all you want," Tumbleweed says, though Blankton's made no effort to shout. "Outside it's a different story." He covers the prisoner's mouth with duct tape then kneels to remove the ankle bindings. "Not that there's anybody around to hear you. But we're not taking any chances."

Tumbleweed shoves Blankton out the back kitchen door. Tigerlily follows. It's the first time she's ever guarded anyone with a gun. The first time she's ever guarded anyone at all. *Don't be afraid to use it. Don't be afraid to…* Of course she's afraid. She's never once fired the shotgun Hank gave her.

Whether or not she would shoot the captive is forgotten the moment she steps out into the crisp air of late autumn. Her ski mask prevents the deep inhalations she craves. She raises her free hand to adjust the eye slots, to better see the sapphire blue sky, the deep green of Frazier furs.

"Okay, Martin, we're going to let you wiggle your arms and legs a little," Tumbleweed says. "Don't want you saying we didn't treat you humanely. But don't go gettin' any crazy notions. Wiggle, shake, do whatever you got to do to keep the circulation going. But make a run for it and—" he lifts his hand even with his eye and points his index finger as if firing a gun—"pow!"

Tumbleweed unwinds the fabric around Blankton's hands, neatly rolling and tucking it until it resembles a plump donut.

A commotion overhead draws her attention. Squinting up into the bright sky, she sees several crows chasing a hawk.

"No!" Tumbleweed shouts. Blankton grabs the bottom of her ski mask and jerks it up. Tumbleweed grabs the gun from her hand.

Blankton seems as startled as she is. He has but a few seconds to study her face, but he does it as if intent on memorizing every crevice and wrinkle. Tumbleweed wallops him on the head with the butt of the gun. In slow motion, Blankton slumps forward and slides to the ground.

"God damn!" Tumbleweed says as they look down at the motionless body.


FOR BACK SUPPORT Elizabeth's brought a chair from the kitchen. Trillium and Waterlily sit on the parlor floor, knees to chin, hands clasping chipped mugs of hot chocolate. Palmetto, also holding a mug, paces. As usual, he wears his Atlanta Braves hat backward. His dark beard has become scruffier, his eyes antagonistic, not at all the friendly ones Elizabeth encountered during the drive from Asheville.

The seating arrangement reminds her of when she taught Sunday school and children clustered at her feet. Another life, those years married to Wendell. Even her own farm and store seem like distant memories, as are Mary's visitations.

"We've got to get him to a doctor," Waterlily says.

"We can't," Palmetto says. "For the same reason you couldn't go. And look at you. You're doing fine. Tumbleweed's up there doing his magic. I said from the start—would anyone listen?"

Trillium directs her remark at him. "We have to accept that this is where things stand, so we have no choice but—"

Elizabeth puts her index finger to her lips. "Shhh." She points at the open heating grate overhead.

"Maybe he ought to hear the truth," Palmetto says. He lifts his chin and shouts toward the ceiling, "He doesn't have any friends. Nobody out there gives a shit about Martin Blankton. Gotta remember to tell Tumbleweed to write a poem about that. No-bod-y gives a fuck about Mar-tin Blank-ton's bad luck."

"We don't know that," Waterlily says. "It's not even been twenty-four hours." She takes a handful of miniature marshmallows from a plastic bag on the floor and drops them into her cup of hot chocolate. "His wife, his—somebody's got to know he didn't make it to the hunting lodge."

"You mean his ex-wife," Trillium says.

"The owner of the lodge," Waterlily says. "You'd think he knows."

"I told you it ain't gonna work." This, of course, from Palmetto.

Trillium unwinds her long legs and stands to face him. She's a good six inches taller. "Man, stop riding that horse!" She steps away from Palmetto, lifts a heavy oak log from the woodpile, drops it on sputtering coals.

"Even if the bastard's all right," Palmetto finally says, "and nothing worse than a bad headache comes of this, it doesn't matter. Everything's too fucked up. So we get a few people worried about the water they drink. There's still the oceans. Temperatures rising, ice melting. We're talking global crisis here, and you think a document getting released is going to matter? Big whoop!"

Trillium points her index finger accusingly. "So why didn't you join a group that is planning to bomb—to bomb, say, Duke Energy or Monsanto?"

"Come on, guys," Waterlily says, "we know in the scheme of things it's a small gesture. We're here because, because… This alone isn't going to change the course of history. But unless somebody keeps drawing attention to the problem…" She picks up the plastic bag of marshmallows. "Speaking of the problem, who bought this? It's what ends up in that trash vortex out in the Pacific."

"Yeah," Palmetto says, "that very bag is on the way to being part of the fifty-third Wonder of the World. Some entrepreneur's gonna charter cruise ships to go see the sight. Then deliver more trash, make it an enormous monument to global consumerism. Before you know it they'll be building condos on it all. Villa de Plastica—how's that for a name? On the Isle de Plastica."

"You think marshmallows should come in a can?" Trillium asks defensively. "You do the shopping next time."

All the while Elizabeth merely listens. She's already done her part in wrecking the operation. She's an old lady who couldn't help but look up at noisy crows.

HANDS FREED, Blankton holds the cup of water to his lips and drinks noisily, while Trillium, Tumbleweed, and Elizabeth, all wearing ski masks, look on. "You might be interested to know," Trillium tells him, "the water you just drank comes from the Cape Fear River."

Blankton's face turns pale. He coughs, as if trying to regurgitate what he drank.

Tumbleweed places his mouth beside the captive's ear. "Fuckin' scary, ain't it, Martin? Bet you drink bottled water. People over there—are you sure minerals like selenium or mercury don't end up in their wells? What's it to you if it leads to malformed fish? Infant mortality? Cancer?"

The prisoner refuses to drink any water for the rest of the day. Or the next.

~~~

EVERYONE EXCEPT WATERLILY, who's keeping guard upstairs, sits around the kitchen table over a lunch of canned tomato soup and grilled Velveeta cheese sandwiches. The mood is despondent. Three days have passed since the kidnapping. Palmetto and Waterlily just returned from Bryson City and reported that, according to their contact in Raleigh, Blankton's disappearance still hasn't made the news.

Elizabeth slowly whirls her spoon around the edge of the soup bowl. They'll think the idea's ridiculous. *You're the person Mary trusted,* Angelica—uh, Waterlily—told her. It could make a difference. No, she already anticipates a mocking response from Palmetto. But Waterlily also said, *We're going to need your maturity, your voice.* Maturity comes from experience. It's about having the ability to make connections the young might not make. She takes a deep breath.

"The thought occurs to me," she says, "I'm thinking that as long as he's here…you know, and the temperature's mild—"

"Thanks to a warming planet," Palmetto interrupts. He has a habit of signaling mockery by raising his right eyebrow.

She ignores the comment. "Instead of keeping him in a dark room and taking him outside for a few minutes of exercise every day, he could do with some—I guess you could call it outdoor education." She's thinking about the way Mary spoke to women at the farm. "He's already seen my face anyway. I could go without the ski mask, to put him more at ease. That would be important, putting him at ease. Maybe I can remind him of the beauty of the natural world."

Palmetto smirks. "And bring about an epiphany, huh? That's what you're imagining? And I do mean imagining. You work your hocus-pocus and he says, 'Why yes, I'll do the right thing.'"

Elizabeth defiantly lifts her chin. "I'm not that naïve. But it makes more sense than just letting him vegetate up there. I'd carry the gun, of course."

Palmetto raises his right eyebrow again. "Yeah, we know how effective she is with a gun."

"Cut it out," Trillium tells him. To the others: "What'll it hurt?"
~~~

Tumbleweed says, "I could stay nearby to make sure he doesn't try anything."

An hour later Elizabeth, gun in her right hand, steers Blankton with her left. She and Tumbleweed already trampled a patch of waist-high grass in the former garden, spread out a plastic sheet, and unrolled two sleeping bags, about five feet apart. At Palmetto's insistence Blankton will lie on a sleeping bag, hands still bound. At Elizabeth's insistence, once he's situated, she'll remove the duct tape covering his mouth so they can engage in conversation.

First, she must persuade him to listen, as Mary urged women to listen. By herself, though, she lacks Mary's charisma, so she'll have to sound like a force to be reckoned with.

"Lie down," she orders Blankton when they get to the cleared area. "On your back."

He looks at the revolver in her hand, then into her face, as if evaluating whether she'll use it. His eyes dart behind her, to Tumbleweed, ski mask over his face, leaning against the frame of the back door.

"I said, lie down. On your back."

He drops to his knees, then turns and twists his body until he's stretched out supine. Holding the gun in her right hand, she rips the tape from his mouth with the left.

"Ouch, damn you!" He brings chin to shoulder, rubs his mouth against his jacket sleeve in a soothing motion.

She considers the pain of pulling off Band-Aids. "Sorry," she says. She steps back and drops to the other sleeping bag, far enough away to prevent his destabilizing her with any sudden movement. She sits with ankles crossed, knees bent.

The daytime temperature has hovered at around fifty degrees. Overhead, feathery cirrus clouds float across a dazzling blue sky. The kind of day she'd be climbing the ridge behind the farm, Jezebel at her heels. Feeling when reaching the bald's pinnacle like she stands on top of the world, gazing down at this beautiful planet.

"Listen," is all she can think to say, sounding less confident than intended.

"What to?" A smart-ass tone. He stares up at her through smudgy horn-rimmed glasses, as if calculating her weakness. All the while shifting his gaze toward Tumbleweed over by the house.

She straightens her posture, tries harder to achieve an authoritative tone. "I said listen."

"How can I listen if I don't know what I'm supposed to hear?"

"You want your mouth taped again? Do as I say. Just…just listen."

He heaves an impatient sigh.

If she wants him to listen, she needs to be quiet. But the silence seems to stretch out so that less than a minute feels like an hour.

"Do you hear the birds? Aren't their songs lovely?"

"If you say so."

"I can't always recognize them by their songs, but right now… They sing to attract a mate, to mark their territory. Sometimes they signal a reason to be afraid. I've heard them warn each other. I'd like to think, though, that sometimes they sing just because they appreciate the beauty around them."

This time she remains quiet long enough to let the birds speak for themselves.

What should she say next? Again her tone sounds like a command: "Let yourself feel the breeze."

"If you say so."

This isn't going as expected. She's angry. "Do not think just because you've seen my face—do not assume I'm merely an old woman you can disregard. Now, let yourself feel the breeze."

She's startled by the sudden presence of her father. He stands between two spruce pines, in the gray cotton twill trousers he used to wear to work in the hardware store.

"What are you doing here?" she asks.

"You're forcing me," Blankton says, "with a gun, I might add."

"Not you."

Vernon adjusts his wire-rimmed glasses with his index finger. "Remember the old saying, 'You catch more flies with honey than with vinegar.' Speak kindly. Put down the gun. You don't need it."

He's gone.

Put the gun down? Yes, it's an instrument for killing, and she'd never kill another human being. On the other hand, she admits to herself, she feels a sense of power when holding it. There's something about the fear in Blankton's eyes, behind his bluster of words, when a gun is pushed against his layer of belly fat.

But during her Rome trip she encountered a father different from the man she grew up with. He claims to have gained insight on the Other Side. And what he just said leaves her wondering. *You've become a woman with power,* Betsy Padgett told her in the back room of the Garden of Hesperides. So how does a woman of power function in circumstances like this? Does she need a gun?

Elizabeth places it on the ground beside her.

She and Blankton stare at each other, he lying on his back, hands tied and resting on his belly, she seated cross-legged on the nearby sleeping bag. She sees in him something she didn't notice earlier. Not a man with hardened eyes and angular jaw, but eyes that are puffy, cheeks that are fleshy. Might the arrogant retorts be an act? Just as her aggressive behavior is?

She tries to see herself through his eyes: an older woman with a pleasantly round face and very short faded red-mixed-with-gray hair.

"What—whatever has caused you to turn to violence?" he asks.

"I might ask the same question of you."

"Huh?"

"The violence you—you protect the pillagers. And now look at the shape it's in. Earth. All the destruction. All the scars."

She doesn't want it to happen. But she thinks of the way she loves the mountains and the pond and the mother bear fiercely protective of her cubs, even the crows that eat the seeds in her garden. She thinks of the frog with a leg growing out of its abdomen, of little Tsura. Tears well in her eyes.

"It—it makes me very, very sad. Not for myself. I won't be around to see the end."

His eyes follow the tears sliding down her cheek.

"Hey, Tigerlily, what's going on?" It's Tumbleweed.

"I'll bring him back in a minute," she yells, then turns to Blankton. "We'll return to nature study another time." She smiles down at him. "I don't think you're a bad man. Probably one who's not been challenged—at least not recently—to think about these things. Here, let's get you up."

Seconds later she escorts him back to the house, leisurely dangling the gun beside her thigh.

BLANKTON'S FIFTH DAY IN CAPTIVITY. He seems to have adjusted to confinement better than members of the cadre. Cabin fever may explain the arguing that's going on, the way they pick at each other like siblings. "Quit humming that fucking song all the time." "How is it that I'm always the one who has to empty his shit?" "I'm tired of canned soup." If Elizabeth doesn't understand their generational lingo or some reference, there's an extended sigh of exasperation. Even from Waterlily.

Taking Blankton outdoors has become an escape for Elizabeth. She directs him to lie on one of the two spread-out sleeping bags. She keeps his hands bound but removes the duct tape covering his mouth.

"I know these aren't the best of circumstances," she says, "but I want you to see the beauty around you. The trees, the sky, the birds. Bio-diversity. A wonderful word, don't you think?"

Blankton nods.

"We're in the heart of one of the most bio-diverse areas of the country. For now. Who knows what's ahead? But we've been letting ourselves feel the breeze, haven't we? It's memory's breath, the breeze is." As if on cue, a gentle wind brushes by, picking up the comforting smell of smoke coming from the chimney.

"The breeze remembers the day you were born. It remembers the day an individual owl was born, the day it died. Wind remembers when this was virgin forest, when the trees spread out their branches to greet each day. Wind remembers when the Mississippi, the Missouri, the Ohio, the Osage, and all the rivers of the world flowed from mountain crags, pure, sparkling. Listen to the wind."

She remains quiet awhile, counting on the elements to speak for themselves. But her neck starts to ache from looking up, her shoulders too. It's an unnatural position, craning the neck. Confident of Tumbleweed's watchful eye, she lies down a few feet from Blankton.

"Look up at the treetops, the dark green of the evergreens against the blue sky. See the way the branches gently sway?" She lifts her arms, moving them back and forth in imitation of the branches. "We take them for granted, you know. The trees. Do you have a tree outside your office window?"

"Yes, several maple trees."

"But do you have *a* tree? A special one that you watch through every season?"

"I wish I had the time."

"I have a tree. It's old, really old, I don't know how old. It stands all alone now. Somebody probably chopped down its relatives to build the barn. The barn's gone, but that old tree, it keeps standing there, all bent over and gnarly. It's got to be lonely, with no family or friends nearby. If I were Irish, I'd think leprechauns live inside its cavity. Created on the third day, trees were, before animals and humans, so the story goes."

"You're not going to get away with this, you know." Spoken not in a threatening way but as if Blankton is genuinely concerned about her welfare.

"You mean abducting you? My own survival isn't my primary goal. The survival of what you see here—the trees and birds and insects. We have to do what we can to save it all from people like you."

"You've got me all wrong. I'm on your side."

"AND FROM RALEIGH," the radio announcer says. "A mystery surrounds the whereabouts of Martin Blankton, director of North Carolina's Department of Environment and Natural Resources. He has not been seen for three days, but was not reported missing until just two hours ago. A woman whose identity has not been released contacted authorities saying she was to join Blankton in Swain County, but he never arrived. She hesitated to report this earlier due to the nature of their relationship. According to his staff, he was going to hunt bear at a friend's lodge in the mountains. Blankton's cell phone has been located in a dumpster in Los Angeles."

"I thought it was strange, him going hunting without a gun," Trillium says.

"An affair?" Tumbleweed mutters. "What would a woman see in him?"

"He has power," Waterlily says. "Men with power, they—the head of environmental studies at school, a skinny guy with—when were aviator glasses frames in style? There's nothing good looking about him at all. But gossip was that he screwed every TA he ever had."

"A man needs more than a title."

"Don't bet your life on it."

# Chapter 21

RILLIUM'S UPSTAIRS READING her pulp fiction while guarding The Blankton Suite. In the parlor Elizabeth and Tumbleweed sit on kitchen chairs near the warmth of the fireplace. Despite EON rules against disclosing personal history—but who's to enforce the rules?—he's been telling her about growing up in Mobile.

He leans forward in the chair, hands clasped between spread legs. "My high school biology teacher kept a few live animals in the classroom. He liked me a lot and put me in charge of feeding them. Mice for the black snake, insects for the toads and lizards. That's how I discovered my love for animals."

Elizabeth understands the teacher's high regard. There's something about Tumbleweed's earnestness and gentle spirit. Incongruent, though, with his earlier advice not to hesitate to use the gun. And he was the one who hit Blankton over the head and knocked him out.

"Is that what inspired you to get involved with EON? The animals?"

"Yeah, partly." He sits up straight and flashes a broad smile. "I'll bet you don't know the official state reptile of Alabama. It's the Alabama red-bellied turtle. It's endangered though. This sounds unrelated, but I've read about languages disappearing, the ones spoken by just a few people who live in really remote parts of the world. For me it's all connected, endangered animals and disappearing languages. When a language dies off, a history dies too. And memory. And I think about the red-bellied turtle. When it's gone, there won't be any trace of red-bellied turtle history. Or memory.

"The American wood stork too. It all makes—"

A sputter, a clank. The near-death rattle of the Impala's engine shutting down. The slam of car doors. Soon Waterlily and

Palmetto burst in the door, letting in a blast of cold air. "Quick, turn on the radio."

Tumbleweed and Tigerlily rush to the kitchen.

"…Carolina's Department of Environment and Natural Resources, as a hostage. The governor has agreed to the group's demands that the following statement be sent through print, public airways, and electronic media:

"'Water is essential to human survival. Martin Blankton has failed to uphold his fiduciary responsibilities by placing the state's water, and hence the public's health, in jeopardy. Factories that poured their byproducts into our waterways have been allowed to escape their cleanup responsibilities by declaring bankruptcy. Coal powered electric plants are allowed to dispose of toxic coal ash slurry and fly ash in ponds that seep into waterways and wells. Last year the Department of Environment and Natural Resources carried out a study documenting the impact of sludge ponds on the health of children whose drinking water comes from wells. This study discloses elevated rates of still-births, genetic abnormalities, and premature deaths. Yet, under pressure by power companies, joined by agribusiness and manufacturers, Martin Blankton has not released the document to the public.

"'Our organization demands that the entire study documenting the health status of children living in areas where well and city water have been compromised be made public. Until that occurs we will continue to hold Martin Blankton.'

"The governor says his confidence in Martin Blankton is unshakable. The FBI denies it has any record of an organization called Friends of Water."

"IT'S TOO COLD TO LIE on the ground, Marty." By day eight Elizabeth's taken to calling him Marty; he calls her Tiger. His hands are bound together, so she positions one of the chairs behind him and steadies him as he drops onto it.

A strange sight it is: a man and woman wearing winter jackets, sitting stiffly on kitchen chairs placed about four feet apart. They both face an overgrown clearing, beyond it a dense forest of leafless deciduous trees and stately evergreens.

Elizabeth still brings the gun along, but mostly for the benefit of whoever may be watching. She places it on the ground nearby.

"Any news?" he asks.

"No, not anything more than what I've already told you. But then, all we have is a radio and information from the ones who go into town. I'm sure that by now TV and newspapers are carrying more. My, it's a beautiful day, isn't it? Crystal clear."

He looks around, inhales deeply. "Yes. Yes, it is."

"You know, I grew up where there's no winter. No, you don't know. In Florida we called it winter, but it wasn't really. I've come to love the change in seasons. Like right now. The crisp air. We've usually had snow by now. In the mountains. Of course, I hope our demands are met before bad weather sets in."

"Where does it come from?"

"Where does what come from?"

"Your courage. Where does it come from? The others—I won't use the word *foolhardy,* but at their age I never considered what could go wrong. I did some really stupid things. But you—what's made you risk everything? For water."

A hint of a laugh. "Risk everything? My courage? I had no choice."

"We always have a choice."

"You're one to speak of choices! The crisis—for me recognizing the fragility of the planet wasn't instinctive, like it is for some people." She's thinking of Angelica. "I had to be shown. And I had to pay attention to the voices. The voices of prophets, I guess you could call them, and finally to the voice of Earth herself. Once that happened, once I paid attention, I couldn't help…I guess you could say I didn't choose this cause; it chose me. I have no courage."

For a while they're both lost in thought. "The life cycle," she finally says, "that's what winter reminds me of. Everything dies. Eventually. A sad thought, isn't it, that we all end up compost?"

"Mmm, it'll take awhile. Assuming your body is buried by an undertaker, put in a casket then a vault." Though they sit in the vast out-of-doors, his slight drawl and baritone voice convey a sense of sharing an intimate conversation in a cozy den. "Now if you want it tossed over there"—he motions toward the forest with his head—"then it'll decompose more quickly."

"Not really a comforting thought."

"Right now some things are just dormant. Bears hibernating, for example. Reptiles. They're beginning brumation. It's not quite hibernating. They wake up to drink now and then." The extent of his knowledge impresses her.

"Any idea what happens now that the earth's getting warmer? Does it throw off the schedules of animals that hibernate or…or…what's the verb for brumation?" She takes her gaze off a vulture soaring the distant sky to look at Blankton.

"Brumate. I wouldn't be surprised."

"Those electric power plants, the ones that burn coal, the ones you've not been monitoring very carefully—don't you ever worry about their effect on the environment?"

He draws in a deep breath, releases it slowly. "Sure. But what your people don't take into account is public demand. Electricity to dry their clothes and run air conditioners, enough hot water to take a ten-minute shower, run their dishwashers. A long list, I'm afraid."

"I understand your predicament."

"No, Tiger, I don't think you do. Nobody does. I doubt your associates would believe this. After my master's in biology I got a doctorate in administration. Had this crazy notion I could make more of a contribution." His attempt at laughter is more an exhalation than a chuckle. "Actually I took the job with the state because of my concern for the environment. Thought, ah, here I'll be able to make a difference. You know, I used to spend a lot of time outdoors. Hiked. Even rode my bicycle to work." He looks down at his rotund torso. "As you can see, I gave it up."

"Where was this?"

"Over near the coast, not far from Wilmington. I care—I worry about the ocean getting too warm for marine life." He turns toward her, raising and lowering his bound hands to count off each concern. "About it rising. About water getting contaminated. About carbon emissions that are warming the planet. I care about all these things. But…but there are pressures."

Their chairs face the clearing, but they've turned their bodies toward each other, he pleading with his eyes to be understood, she communicating with hers a desire to understand.

"The governor appoints me, but he had to have the power company's support to win the election, so he tells me I can't be too strict with them. And the timber companies, they furnish a lot of jobs, and jobs are important to the economy. People need jobs, and if there are too many restrictions on companies, they'll move to another state."

"And this study we want made public?"

"I had no choice. Senator McWilliams made a personal visit. Lobbyists put the squeeze on him. I was told to bury it. Ordered to. I love the planet as much as anybody, but if I did my job the way you and your people think it ought to be done, the economy of the state would collapse."

She doesn't know what comes over her. She rises from her chair and steps over to Martin. She leans down and kisses him. Right on the lips.

ATOP A GIANT STUMP, Elizabeth has placed miniature pine cones, a rock, a small pile of dried leaves, two gray feathers, and a cup of water. She sits cross-legged on the ground beside the collection, palms open, receptive.

"Please, Blessed Mother, you yourself once told me that sometimes the supernatural works. I know the women let you down, but these young people who are taking up the cause. They need—*we* need your intervention."

Mary's never come at Elizabeth's bidding, preferring it seems, to spring up unexpectedly. Or, in the case of the appearances, according to Mary's own schedule. But the situation is becoming urgent. The kidnapping's not going according to plan.

Elizabeth has no idea what kind of intervention would further the cause. Maybe Mary does. If she's listening.

ELIZABETH, ALONG WITH TRILLIUM and Palmetto, sits at the kitchen table, ears turned toward the radio on the floor. "An update on the kidnapping of Martin Blankton, head of the

Department of Environment and Natural Resources. The group calling itself Friends of Water claims to have Blankton in an undisclosed location and has demanded the release to the public of a report documenting the effects of compromised water supplies on the growth and development of children. However, the governor says no such report exists and demands that Blankton be freed.

"Meanwhile, the woman who was to meet Blankton at a mountain cabin has been identified as Kitty Van Doran, a media consultant to the department. We take you now outside her residence in Durham, where reporters have gathered. John Westminster, tell us, what is Miss Van Doran saying about their relationship?"

"Leslie, Kitty Van Doran has not left her house since Blankton's abduction came to light. A friend of hers, Carla Longstreet, has been staying with her and taking her pet schnauzer for walks. She told reporters that Miss Van Doran had been recovering from a painful breakup and only recently began seeing Blankton. That's all she will say."

Elizabeth feels a twinge of jealousy. She pictures this Kitty Van Doran, thirtyish and only able to engage in shallow conversation. Probably with bleached blond hair and too much eye makeup. Seducer of men with power. No, that's unkind. What woman wouldn't enjoy Marty's companionship?

TEN DAYS HAVE PASSED since the kidnapping. The weather's shifted, winds sweep cold air southward from the Great Plains. Ice forms on window panes and frigid drafts swirl across the floor.

Every morning Elizabeth is the first to rise. Her steps on creaking floorboards often awaken whoever's keeping watch outside Blankton's door. She lights the fire in the fireplace then follows the path into a sheltered place among the mountain laurel and squats. Or in reverse order, depending upon the urgency. She's growing accustomed to instant coffee and canned entrees: ravioli, beef stew, chicken chow mein. Twice, when Angelica drove to Bryson City for supplies, she returned with fresh chicken parts and hamburger. Palmetto complained about the expense. Until he tasted how Elizabeth, with a warped skillet, can transform a few simple ingredients into a savory meal.

It's become too cold to stretch out on sleeping bags or sit on kitchen chairs behind the house. Over Trillium's and Tumbleweed's objections Elizabeth and Marty take daily brisk walks around the parameter of the cleared area. During two days of solid rain, the two of them play twenty questions in the Blankton Suite. Palmetto grumbles that their laughter compromises the demands of Friends of Water.

Elizabeth wonders how long the group will be able to live under the same roof and continue to work toward a common goal.

TUMBLEWEED HOLDS BACK a long briar vine to keep it from slapping Elizabeth across the face. "Do you have any idea what it's like for a city guy like me to be stuck out here? I thought I'd like it, but dear God…"

He, Trillium, and Elizabeth are making their way up a steep trail, through a stand of poplars. Dried leaves crunch beneath their boots. Back at the house Waterlily keeps guard outside Blankton's door. Palmetto is averse to exercise.

"The silence," Tumbleweed says. "I can't stand it. Give me traffic any day. Cars honking, motorcycles revving. I'm used to people talking out on the sidewalk. It's too quiet here. Except for those damn screech owls." He stops in the path and appeals to Trillium. "You've got to let me go into town. Just once."

"He knoweth not what he asketh," Trillium says. "Everybody's white. It's a small town and you'd stand out like a sore thumb."

"Think you don't? How many other girls your height are walking down the sidewalk?"

"I slump." She slaps him affectionately on the back.

The forest ends abruptly, its edges lined with aged rhododendron, their long grayish woody stalks leafless except for ends exposed to light. Ahead the gradual slope of a bald is bathed in sunshine.

"Race you," Trillium says and takes off running uphill through tall grass. Tumbleweed has no choice but to run too, his strides no match for her long legs. Elizabeth maintains her own pace, smiling over their agility and energy. Of the Group of Five these two seem to get along best.

She sympathizes with Tumbleweed's uneasiness. But for her the issue is unrelated to extended periods of silence or night noises. It's confusion over her feelings for Marty. He is the captive, and she's much too fond of him. When his betrayal of the public trust and the resulting harm to children's health is exposed, will she be able to stand against him?

Continuing her slow climb up the bald, she considers the way Marty treats her. She can speak her mind forcefully, and he comes back with equal vigor, respectful of her opinion.

Much in recent years has bolstered her self-confidence. The success of the farm and the store. The honor of being Mary's mouthpiece. Together Mary and Angelica have won her over to a cause. The cry of Earth has stirred her passion. She can see in Marty's eyes and hear in his voice that he likes this version of who she is.

But she's had little experience with men. Sure, Wendell is one, and in college she spent most of a semester hanging out with a rebellious crowd that included four males. Marty, though, has traveled the world. He knows important people. He's well educated. Probably makes a lot of money. What if he's taking advantage of her naiveté and plans to use her affection to escape?

Up ahead, halfway to the top, Trillium breaks stride and abruptly stops next to a rock outcrop. The afternoon sun shines on a flat boulder. She touches its surface, checking for warmth, then lies down on it. She drapes an arm over her eyes to shield them from the sun. Tumbleweed stands beside her, leaning over with hands on his thighs, panting.

By the time Elizabeth catches up, he's sitting on the boulder next to Trillium's stretched-out body, his arms dangling over bent knees, gazing out over the vista.

"Miles and miles and miles," he says, sweeping an arm across the horizon. "All those ridges, one after another. What have I been thinking, feeling homesick for the city? Kids back home, a lot of them have never seen beauty like this. That's why I'm involved in this project. To protect all this."

Elizabeth pushes thoughts of Blankton aside, sits down next to Tumbleweed, and turns her face to take in the warmth of the sun. No one speaks for a while.

"What if it's been destroyed?" she finally asks. Tumbleweed looks over at her questioningly. "The report. What if it's been destroyed?"

"That copy, maybe," he says, "especially now that it's come to light. But four other people were cc'ed. Saw it myself. Blankton's secretary, it was in her file drawer."

"What were you doing in her file drawer?"

"I was working for a janitorial service that cleans some of the government buildings. Guess you could call me a spy."

"Why didn't you just take it?"

"Could have, but then they'd claim we wrote it ourselves. It's there, the report. I took a picture."

From beneath her protective arm Trillium speaks. "So how are we going to convince them we mean business? Send them an ear?"

"Hmm." Tumbleweed purses his lips, like he's taking the suggestion seriously. "His secretary knows we're telling the truth. We've got her name."

Trillium sits up. "Yeah, but she's a single mom, isn't she? Let's keep her out of this."

"She might decide on her own to come forward."

Trillium stands and stretches. "No. I've got an idea. Let's get him to write a letter. To his second in command—Peter Golder or Golden. Get Ponderosa to release it to the media. Have him write that he now understands that the health of children is more important than companies making money. Tigerlily, you can get him to do it, can't you?"


At the kitchen table, a sheet of paper and a pen in front of him, Blankton sits surrounded by Friends of Water. Palmetto holds a revolver. Elizabeth is the only one not wearing a ski mask.

"I'm going to untie your hands for a little while," she tells him. "You're to write what I say."

Free of the fabric binding his hands, Blankton stretches his arms and hands, wriggles his fingers. He picks up the pen.

"Okay, this is what you're to write: Dear Peter Guilder. Or are you more likely to call him Peter?"

"Just Peter."

She proceeds to dictate, allowing him time to put words on paper. "Friends of Water are demanding that the agency release the complete Unsafe Water Report to the public. As a public servant, I feel an obligation to the families of our communities to make them aware of the health dangers to which they are being exposed. Therefore, I'm instructing you to release the report."

Though no one has mentioned the possibility, Blankton keeps writing then reads aloud, "If you don't, they will kill me. They mean business." Followed by his signature: Martin.

He looks up at Elizabeth, gives her a half-smile and a wink. "This should get some action."

THE EARLY MORNING SUN shines on the back stoop, where Elizabeth continues to write her memories on the yellow pad. She's almost finished telling of Mary's visitations, combining what others described and her own recollections, faint though they be.

The door behind her opens.

"Morning, uh, Tigerlily." Waterlily stands there with two cups of instant coffee. She hands one to her mother and sits down. "It's hard to know," she says after a while, "how all this is going to play out, isn't it? I feel bad for having invited you into this—everything was supposed to fall in place quickly."

"It's not over yet. No matter what happens, I have no regrets."

They sit silently, both clasping the chipped ceramic cups and staring into the woods. "Right now," Waterlily says, "I'm most concerned about—I don't know how to approach this. I'm most concerned about your—about your relationship with Blankton."

"My relationship with…?"

"I know you, Mom, and I've never seen you this way around a man."

Elizabeth pretends not to understand. "Whatever do you mean?"

"We all saw the way he looked up at you when he finished writing that letter. The way you two laugh and the low-tone conversations. He's our bargaining chip, Mom. You can't become buddies with our bargaining chip."

"You've got this all wrong."

"Do I? Like I said, I know you. When's the last time you talked with a man? Besides Hank, of course. Conversations with male customers are like, 'That will be twenty dollars and thirty-four cents.' You're not supposed to fall in love with the hostage."

"Now, look here. I'm not falling in love. I can handle this."

"I can handle this? That's always been my line." Waterlily gives her mother's shoulders a squeeze and grins. "You can't have it."

She stands. "Be careful, Mom. Don't jeopardize our plan." She goes back inside.

Angelica didn't say anything Elizabeth hasn't already thought about. But what's she to do about this stirring inside her?

THE CANNED CHICKEN CHOW MEIN is too salty, the white rice mushy. At least this evening there's a green salad of sorts: a wedge of iceberg lettuce and French dressing, an intense shade of orange derived, no doubt, from a combination of food dyes.

By day thirteen—seventeen if counting those before the kidnapping—meals around the table have become such a time for bickering that everyone now fills their plates then scatters. Waterlily is on guard duty upstairs, where she can eat in silence. Tumbleweed and Trillium have taken their plates in by the fireplace. Palmetto and Elizabeth eat at the kitchen table.

Tumbleweed's words carry from the parlor into the kitchen. "I'm so fucking tired of being cold."

"For all his intellect—" Palmetto speaks and chews at the same time—"you'd think..." He raises his voice to make sure Tumbleweed hears: "You'd think a guy that smart would have thought, duh, it may get cold in November. You packed summer clothes, Dickhead."

"Go fuck yourself," Tumbleweed yells back. "Where I come from we call November autumn. And we have central heat."

"Children, pu-lease cut it out," Elizabeth pleads. "We only need to get along a day or two more." *Oh, Lord, how I sound like my mother,* she's thought several times during recent days. Always pleading for harmony.

"It's perfectly understandable," Trillium says in Tumbleweed's defense. "Who anticipated we'd be here this long?"

"Maybe you could get Blankton to share his clothes," Palmetto says. "The stuff in that duffle bag—looks like he wasn't planning to spend all his time in the sack with that broad."

"Against the Geneva Conventions, wearing a captive's long-johns. And what if I'm taking him outside? Who gets them then? And what about gloves? One for him and one for me?"

Trillium brings her empty plate into the kitchen and puts it in the wash basin. "There's a thrift store in Bryson City." She seems to be speaking to herself. "He could pick up a heavy sweater there, probably gloves and a scarf too. Don't know about long-johns." She repeats what she just said, louder this time so Tumbleweed can hear her in the parlor. "I said there's a thrift store in Bryson City. I'm sure you could buy something warm to wear."

*Why don't you just lick the dish?* Elizabeth's tempted to ask as Palmetto runs a finger around the edge of his plate. She scolds herself for being as ill-tempered as the others.

"Okay, we'll be the ones to go in town tomorrow," Palmetto calls to Tumbleweed. "I doubt it'll hurt for you to be seen one time."

Trillium carries her washed and dried plate over to the cupboard on the wall. "No, he and I will go," she says. "I need to give Ponderosa a personal message to pass on."

Palmetto fingers the bill of his Atlanta Braves cap. "Now wouldn't that be something? A black dude and a girl tall enough to mate with a giraffe showing up together. Think nobody would notice? I say the best combination is us two guys."

But sometime after Elizabeth goes upstairs and snuggles into her sleeping bag, plans change.

It's Tumbleweed and Waterlily who set out in the Impala. To avoid being seen together, she'll drop him off a few blocks from Main Street and pick him up at the same location at noon. He'll buy the clothes and call the contact in Raleigh, who will probably have something to report about Blankton's letter. Meanwhile, Angelica/Waterlily will do the necessary grocery shopping. Trillium's need to send a personal message seems to have been forgotten.

Two dreary days have passed since there's been any Outdoor Education. Two days of drizzling rain and temperatures in the low thirties. On the morning Tumbleweed and Waterlily drive to Bryson City, the clouds lift. By late morning the patch of mountain land on which the abandoned farmhouse stands is bathed in sunshine.

Elizabeth climbs the stairs to The Blankton Suite. Trillium sits beside the door, nose in the same paperback she's been reading the whole two weeks. She holds it up. "If I'd known we were going to be here this long, I'd have brought *War and Peace,* or something else worth reading more than once."

"I thought I'd take Blankton out for some vitamin D." To convince Trillium that taking him outside is a good idea, Elizabeth adds, "Our plan to help him develop more environmental awareness is working. Once he's free and back at work, I'm confident he'll be our ally."

Trillium leans forward in the backless chair, the closed book under her arm. "And what about you? Think you two are buddies for life now? You'd better prepare yourself. Once he's free you'll never see him again."

Elizabeth shrugs her shoulders and reaches for the door handle. "Be that as it may, we'll have accomplished our goal."

"I don't think it's a good idea, taking him outside while the others are gone."

"Palmetto's downstairs. I'll get him to stand guard. Though I really don't think it's necessary anymore."

"Do what you want. I need to go pee anyway."

~~~

EARLIER ELIZABETH BROUGHT out two chairs from the kitchen, placed them four feet apart. Now Marty, hands bound, stands in their usual section of trampled weeds. She grasps his arm, intending only to offer support as his body drops onto a chair. Yet once he's situated, she continues to hold the sleeve of his jacket, until an awkwardness hovers over them. Embarrassed, she clears her throat, lets go of his arm, and sits down in the other chair.

For a while neither speaks. She listens to the forest's melodies and inhales the fragrance of cedar trees. Palmetto sits on the concrete step leading into the kitchen, clipping his fingernails, revolver at his side. He adjusts his ski mask to better see his hands.

"Listen to the woodpecker," Marty says. "Sounds industrious, doesn't it? The opposite of me." He makes a guttural sound bordering on a chuckle. "Can't say I've liked being your prisoner. Or that I like being guarded by someone with a gun. But all this has been—I want you to know in case we don't have time to say goodbye—I want you to know I'm grateful. For the chance to be outside like this. And for your friendship. We'll leave this place friends, won't we?"

"Yes, we will."

"It's also been a good substitute for a disciplined diet. My pants are loose in the waist."

She doesn't bother looking over. Her mind sees his unshaven face, matted down hair, clothes only washed twice. She also pictures how the anger furrows across his brow have disappeared.

"I sensed it in you from the first," she says, facing him, "your love of nature. You just needed reminding."

His chin is lifted, his gaze on the sky above. His bound hands rest in his lap. "It's not going to make any difference, you know. So the report's made public. Media will blast it all over the place for a few days, startle everyone, but then the news cycle will move on to something else." He turns his head, squints as he looks at her. "The sun behind you makes you look like you have
~~~

a halo. Saint Tiger…If my hands were free, I'd wipe those worry lines off your face."

*If my hands were free.* Years have passed since anyone has touched her in tenderness. *Saint Tiger. If my hands were free. If my hands were free. Think you two are buddies for life now? Once he's free you'll never see him again.* If she untied his hands, instead of wiping away the worry lines, he might just take off running. Then Palmetto would shoot, maybe even kill him.

She leans forward, propping elbows on her knees, cupping her chin in the palms of her hands. She looks straight ahead into the forest. "You're probably right," she says. "About the media, the public's short attention span. Does that mean we're all supposed to—are we just supposed to pretend nothing's wrong? Leave everything for another generation to worry about? Que sera, sera?"

Another moment of awkward silence. She tugs at a loose thread on her down jacket. He leans back in the chair and closes his eyes. "These kids," he says, "I'm not sure what motivates them. Optimism, I guess. They see the mess our generation's left things in and think they can turn it all around. They'll learn otherwise." He raises his bound hands to scratch his bearded chin. "I'm not sure what I'll do when I get back. Assuming I make it."

"You're a good man. I know that. But—what I want from our times out here—I want you to be courageous. It's not enough anymore to say it's all complicated. That's to accept defeat."

*If my hands were free. If my hands were free.* She imagines what Marty's touch might feel like. She'd unbind his hands. He'd reach over and brush fingertips across her lips, bring his face toward—

Faint swishing noises. A rustling among the nearest trees. The woodpecker's hammering, the crows' caws—forest voices become eerily still. She straightens her posture and looks around.

"Run!" Palmetto shouts.

From behind tree trunks and thick brush, six men in camouflage storm the clearing. They carry military weapons.

Her gun. Where did she leave it? The instant she leans over to pick it up off the ground, a shot rings out. She gasps for breath and falls to the ground.

Hands bound prayer-like, Marty drops to his knees and throws his body on hers. His "Nooo!" rings through the forest.

# A Vision

*And I shall dwell in the house of the Lord forever. And I shall dwell… Do not weep for me. Weep for the land. Our people have sacrificed their young men. All that we hold dear has perished. The South is left with nothing. Nothing but honor. As I now die with honor, Father Walter has reminded me. The noose, oh, God, it encircles my neck. Please don't let me drop. Holy Mary, Mother of God, pray for us sinners, now and in the hour of our death. Amen.*

# Chapter 22

A POSTMARK FROM AN ARIZONA TOWN I've never heard of. The return address a name I don't recognize. But as sure as water flows downhill, those are my brother's heavy pen strokes on the box's address label: straight up and down with few curves, jerky.

Any minute Russ will get home from work. He knows little about my past, other than that I grew up on a Virginia farm then lived with my mother in North Carolina. And that my parents divorced when I was in high school. Early in our relationship he asked how I got the faint inch-long scar that starts at the corner of my mouth. He accepted my explanation that I fell off my bicycle when I was a girl. He doesn't probe.

The box is big. Our house is small. The two narrow closets are overflowing. Russ will immediately recognize anything out of the ordinary.

I rush from the house, the heavy box awkward in my arms, to our garden shed at the edge of the lot. I place a tarp on the damp floor, and, as if the box were a gift—which it in fact is—I wrap the tarp around it.

The next morning, with Russ off to work, I throw on a wool sweater and head for the shed. The day is dreary, moisture from the previous night's storm dripping from bare branches. Stepping onto the dirt floor of the shed, I turn on the single bare bulb hanging from a wire. With a knife I cut the tape securing the box top, lift the four cardboard flaps, and gaze upon…

Paper. A box full of paper. Newspaper articles, photographs, scraps on which notes have been hastily written, letters typed on official looking stationary, thin notebooks from which pages have been torn. Three yellow legal pads, my mother's writing filling the lines. Atop everything, a letter:

Dear Sis,

I don't want to risk blowing your cover, but know you'd be furious if I threw away Mom's papers. I finally sold her farm and have been getting rid of the house's contents. This box was in the attic. Burn everything if you want. I doubt you'll do that, though, since you were the only person who understood her.

You'll be surprised to learn that I'm getting married. Yes, I'm finally tying the knot. I wish you could come to the wedding (June 10th) but know it's impossible. Marissa's not at all like Mom, which is important to me. For one thing she agrees with Holy Scripture that the man is head of the household. More important, she's sane.

Love,

Randy

P.S. Any suggestions on a way to give you your share from the sale without leading the Feds to your doorstep?

I REMOVE AN OLD FOLDING STOOL from a hook on the wall, test it to make sure the canvas hasn't rotted. Outside the rain resumes. What begins as faint pings against the tin roof turns into a loud clatter. I withdraw a handful of papers from beneath Randy's note and push the box under the worktable to protect it from water leaking through the roof. As I sort the papers, an occasional raindrop falls on my face, blending with my tears.

*She was, dear child in my womb, a grandmother deserving your admiration and affection, a woman whose courage is your legacy: Elizabeth Pierson Mattison McNair.*

# Acknowledgments

MY SINCERE THANKS to friends who read various stages of this story's development: Carol Talmage, Sally Schoen, Jeanne Charters Restivo, Celia Miles, and Jeanne Franklin. Against the advice of most of them, Mary Surratt remained. Several times I tried to take her out but she refused to be excluded. During the book's earliest development, Kemper Bornman lent her understanding about human nature and women's wisdom. All who loved Kemper continue to miss her warmth and laughter.

Of course, none of my thoughts would be put to paper were it not for the love and support of my husband and best friend, James Newton Poling, who has been listening to me talk about these characters for at least ten years. His love for Earth and all its creatures continues to inspire me.

## About the Cover Artist

JERALD POPE writes, draws, and paints because he believes:

(1) Representative art reveals things about the artist, the subject, and the viewer that photography, for example, cannot;
(2) Art ducks around the Corner of Logic to tell stories, suggest solutions, sooth souls, and delight in most unexpected ways; and
(3) If purpose there is, then his is found with pencil in hand.

He currently lives in the mountains near Asheville, NC, with a wife, a dog, and a studio where he happily continues to write, draw, paint and occasionally do commissioned work.